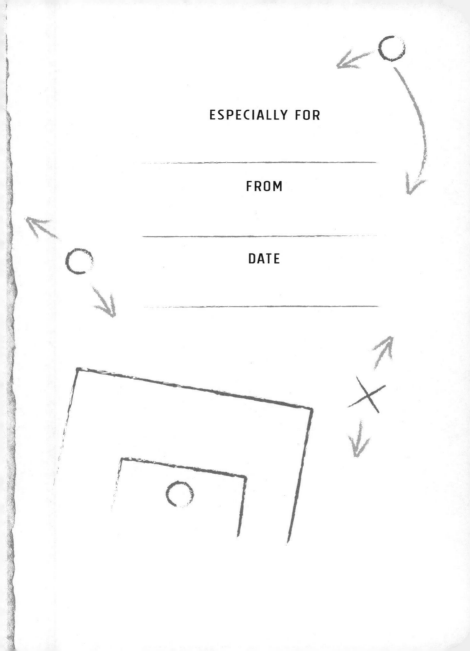

ESPECIALLY FOR

_____

FROM

_____

DATE

_____

GOD'S PLAYBOOK
FOR DADS

BIBLE WISDOM FOR
FATHERS FROM THE GREATEST
COACH OF ALL TIME

QUENTIN GUY

BARBOUR BOOKS
An Imprint of Barbour Publishing, Inc.

Published by Barbour Books, an imprint of Barbour Publishing, Inc., 1810 Barbour Drive, Uhrichsville, Ohio 44683, www.barbourbooks.com

Our mission is to inspire the world with the life-changing message of the Bible.

Member of the
Evangelical Christian
Publishers Association

Printed in China.

CONTENTS

INTRODUCTION

Being a dad is a lot like coaching a team. This book is your clipboard, a game plan for success. Most game plans divide into two parts, offense and defense. There's a time and place for each. When you're on offense, you're engaging with your kids—playing, listening, disciplining, supporting. When you're on defense, you're working on yourself, preparing for your interactions with them. Both will evolve over time as your interactions with your kids force you to evaluate your approach.

You'll find eight major sections in this book called strategy sessions, each of which give an overview of the topic at hand. Within each strategy session, you'll find at least one playbook that contains a group of specific topics to ponder. You can go through the book consecutively or in any order you choose.

Congrats on choosing to get in the game and bench passivity. Of course, there are situations you can't be totally prepared for, and a lot of good parenting happens on the fly, meaning you must respond to events as they occur and deal with consequences as they arise.

Do this, but with a spiritual foundation based on scripture. Your success regarding what happens on the fly is affected by your behind-the-scenes work in Bible reading, prayer, and your everyday interactions with your kids. It's a lot to manage, but don't worry—with God's help, you've got this.

STRATEGY SESSION 1:

X's AND O's

TAKE A BREATH

> Fatherhood has taught me about unconditional
> love, reinforced the importance of giving back,
> and taught me how to be a better person.
> NAVEEN JAIN

Every one of us has lived in the shadow of our father, whether it was secure and comforting, heartbreaking and frightening, or cast by absence. A father's love can build his child into something special, and his indifference can create a lifelong search for approval.

The reason for that impact is startlingly simple: dads are supposed to be a child's first point of reference for God. Our Father in heaven wants a relationship with us, wants our obedience so He can bless us—but if our earthly fathers don't give us some idea of how good God is, we are in for a rough ride.

That weight is overwhelming—it should be—but with God's help, you will not only bear it, you will succeed in raising kids who know the power of a father's love and who transition successfully to their own relationship with their Maker.

> *Don't worry about anything; instead, pray*
> *about everything. Tell God what you need,*
> *and thank him for all he has done.*
> PHILIPPIANS 4:6 NLT

BACK TO BASICS

*Perfection is not attainable, but if we chase
perfection, we can catch excellence.*
VINCE LOMBARDI

Hall of Fame football coach Vince Lombardi began his first meeting with his new team each season in a legendary way. He held up an oblong spheroid with stripes around each end. "This, gentlemen," he said, "is a football."

Lombardi went back to basics. His men knew what a football was, knew the basics of the game, knew what it was to win and lose—but their coach took nothing for granted. He was determined to get them all on the same page with his vision. He turned a single-minded devotion to excellence into five championships, including the first two Super Bowls.

If you've been a dad for any length of time, you know you can't take anything for granted. You provide your children's introduction to God and model what it is to trust Him. Success depends on how well you understand and follow God's game plan.

*I don't mean to say that I have already achieved
these things or that I have already reached perfection.
But I press on to possess that perfection for
which Christ Jesus first possessed me.*
PHILIPPIANS 3:12 NLT

THE PURSUIT OF HOLINESS

Desire is the key to motivation, but it's determination
and commitment to an unrelenting pursuit of
your goal—a commitment to excellence—that will
enable you to attain the success you seek.
MARIO ANDRETTI

A number of factors influence your ability to succeed as a father, but none is more important than your commitment to holiness. Being holy doesn't mean spending your prefatherhood years cloistered in a monastery, eating once a day, and contemplating your navel. What it means is far more engaged in your everyday life: be God's man in every part of your life.

Holiness is separation from the ways of the world—from its philosophies, practices, traditions that seek self above all else: self-reliance, self-esteem, self-sufficiency. And these days, to show off those things, we take selfies.

However, if you see fatherhood as an opportunity to know God better and to direct a young life toward that same pursuit, it begins to dawn on you: being a dad is holy business, and very few things matter more.

Take heed to yourself and to the doctrine.
Continue in them, for in doing this you will save
both yourself and those who hear you.
1 TIMOTHY 4:16 NKJV

OUT OF CONTROL

We must be willing to let go of the
life we have planned, so as to have
the life that is waiting for us.
E. M. FORSTER

Remember when God gave Adam and Eve dominion over the earth and told them to be fruitful and multiply? Wanting to be in charge isn't a sin; it's part of who God made us to be. But the Fall made it clear that free will and power form a volatile combo. We need some kind of safe container to put this combo in, something that keeps us from pressing the button and blowing up everything.

The key is knowing what you can and can't control. God alone has ultimate control. Your most important decision is whether you're going to acknowledge that and let Him lead you as you go through life. God reminded Cain of the grim prospects of doing anything else. By letting God be God, you'll have perspective on anything life throws at you.

"If you do well, will you not be accepted?
And if you do not do well, sin lies at the door. And its
desire is for you, but you should rule over it."
GENESIS 4:7 NKJV

THE PROVIDER

The greatest legacy one can pass on to one's
children and grandchildren is not money or other material
things accumulated in one's life, but rather a
legacy of character and faith.

BILLY GRAHAM

God made men to be providers. From Eden on, we see that men are meant to take care of their families' essential physical needs—food, shelter, and safety. God made men to work too, and not pursuing work eats at a key part of who God made us to be.

Even though sin and the Fall made work difficult and hard to enjoy, work itself is a good thing. Through it, God gives us a taste of what it's like to create and sustain something valuable. But there is clearly more to being a provider than just bringing home a paycheck. Men are also to provide as husbands and fathers, bringing truth, love, and spiritual values to their families. Like Jesus said, there's more to life than bread. Realizing that truth is where spiritual leadership starts.

*If anyone does not provide for his own, and
especially for those of his household, he has denied
the faith and is worse than an unbeliever.*
1 TIMOTHY 5:8 NASB

HUMILITY TAKES PRACTICE

Humility is not thinking less of yourself;
it's thinking of yourself less.
RICK WARREN

Playing the role of provider is fueled by the practice of humility. *Practice* is the key word, because that's what it takes to be humble. True humility takes effort—not the sweat-of-your-brow kind, but the realize-you're-not-God kind.

It's easy to become prideful about doing the right things— providing for your family, going to kids' ball games, serving at church. But those things are right because God's nature includes provision, involvement, and service.

The real question is, are you doing them for the right reasons? Are you rushing from work to pick up your kids *because* they deserve your support? Are you leaving an important meeting when one of them is in the ER *because* they need your presence? Are you spending time with God every day *because* you can't do all these other things with the right perspective without Him? Humbling yourself before God is the first rule of practicing humility. As Paul said, that's your reasonable service.

*"It shall not be so among you; but whoever desires
to become great among you, let him be your servant."*
MATTHEW 20:26 NKJV

THE NEW MATH STILL SAYS
TO COUNT YOUR BLESSINGS

Christ frequently gives us the desires
of our heart, though not at the peculiar
time we desired, but at a better time.
ROBERT MURRAY MCCHEYNE

All the hard work it takes to be a dad is worth it. For all the money you spend on Christmas and birthday parties and piano lessons and baseball gloves, the scales can be balanced by a smile or a hug, or little eyes opening wide with delight just because you're home. For all the angst, arguments, math homework, and dented fenders, you're back in black with just one inside joke or even a hard-won "Thank you."

You probably never imagined being a good dad would be so difficult. But you probably didn't anticipate how great it would be either. You can't anticipate the love you can feel until you hold that baby yourself. With every loving sacrifice you make for your kids, you do a fine imitation of your heavenly Father, who gave His very best for you.

Every good and perfect gift is from above,
coming down from the Father of the heavenly lights,
who does not change like shifting shadows.
JAMES 1:17 NIV

LOVING LIKE GOD

I want the love that cannot help but love,
loving like God, for the very sake of love.
A. B. SIMPSON

L ove is often greatly misunderstood. It is so much more than gushy emotions and warm fuzzies. Love is both youthful bonfire and the fireplace embers of later years. But most often, love looks like something completely different—especially with kids. It looks like Band-Aids on skinned knees or midnight hours on Christmas Eve putting together a bike. It looks like getting vomited on and smiling, and like handing over the keys and saying, "Be safe."

Kids force you to ask, *How can I love someone I don't like right now?* The answer may surprise you: when you do, you're loving a lot like God does. Kids need a ton of patience and tolerance, and so do you. God gives you that kind of love every day—it's what made Him give His Son to save you and what has kept you on His mind every day since. That's the kind of love you can more fully appreciate when you become a father.

God demonstrates His own love toward us,
in that while we were still sinners, Christ died for us.
ROMANS 5:8 NKJV

A STATE OF GRACE

*A state of mind that sees God in everything is
evidence of growth in grace and a thankful heart.*
CHARLES FINNEY

You know your job as a dad is to recognize your kids' mistakes, to try to prevent them from happening, and to ensure appropriate consequences when they do. But is it realistic to think you'll catch everything? After all, you know you got away with things as a kid.

That's where God comes in. He sees everything, so in the long run, we get away with nothing. But more importantly, He knows what's in every heart. That's why the best thing you can do to prevent clean getaways for your kids is to teach them about who God is. On one hand, no one gets away with anything. On the other, God has made a way for us to be forgiven and to move forward and please the One who sees and knows everything.

There's a name for that: grace.

*[God] said to [Paul], "My grace is sufficient for you,
for my power is made perfect in weakness." Therefore I
will boast all the more gladly about my weaknesses,
so that Christ's power may rest on me.*
2 CORINTHIANS 12:9 NIV

GLORY IN WEAKNESS

Real true faith is man's weakness
leaning on God's strength.
DWIGHT L. MOODY

N o man likes to think of himself as weak. We think of the great saints of the Bible, such as Paul, who repeatedly endured thirty-nine lashes, and David, who refused to kill Saul in the cave, and wonder, *Could I do that if I had to?*

Remember, though, how Paul and David saw their challenges. Paul went to jail gladly because his mission was anywhere God put him. David killed Goliath because he knew that even the most imposing warrior had no chance against the Lord. But they knew their accomplishments and strengths weren't enough to do the work God had for them.

Being a dad is like that. You'll feel angry and frustrated at times. Who has the strength to raise kids well and never lose his cool or feel defeated? None of us. But even when that happens, the game's not over. Let go of trying to be Superman in every situation and let God's strength be yours. He won't let you down.

I am well content with weaknesses, with insults,
with distresses, with persecutions, with difficulties,
for Christ's sake; for when I am weak, then I am strong.
2 CORINTHIANS 12:10 NASB

LIKE A ROCK

God works powerfully, but for the
most part gently and gradually.
JOHN NEWTON

Never underestimate the power you have in your kids' lives.
When they're little, they depend on you for their most basic
needs. As they get older, they become quietly desperate for
your approval and affirmation. When they're out on their own,
they still need your wisdom. And when they have their own kids,
they need your emotional support and friendship.

You should always wield your power as a dad wisely. A show
of force—a physical threat or verbal barrage—may demonstrate
that you're stronger or quicker witted (for the time being), but
it only reveals something weak and cold in you.

The best use of your influence is in patiently playing the
long game. God is working His will and ways in you over time,
and He is using you to do the same for your children. When your
relationship with Him reflects that steady, stable approach, you'll
show the same with your kids.

*"Everyone who hears these sayings of Mine,
and does not do them, will be like a foolish
man who built his house on the sand."*
MATTHEW 7:26 NKJV

CREATE A CULTURE OF PEACE

A peaceful home is as sacred as any chapel or cathedral.
BIL KEANE

Although it's good to get your kids to read the Bible daily or listen only to Christian music, what they do is not going to make your home a Christian one. That's defined by what parents do, not children. And you as the dad set the tone.

Training your kids up in the Lord doesn't mean getting them to march lockstep like good little soldiers in Christian apparel. It means living your own life by what Jesus called "the unforced rhythms of grace" (Matthew 11:29 MSG). If your kids see you resting in Jesus, giving Him your anxieties, reading your Bible, and bringing up what God is teaching you in regular conversation, they'll see that following God isn't a command performance but a way of life.

Your authority flows from God, so knowing Him yourself makes you a conduit for His blessings. Your kids will see that the peace you have comes because you have a real relationship with Jesus. That makes Christ inviting for them, and His peace will settle on your home.

If it is possible, as far as it depends on you,
live at peace with everyone.
ROMANS 12:18 NIV

IS THIS THING ON?

"My son looks at me out of nowhere and says,
'Dad, I'm going to be a doctor.' " It was like, 'Yes,
yes, yes!' Then he said, 'Or a dinosaur.' "
MICHAEL JR.

Almost everyone likes to laugh. Laughing releases tension, lightens burdens, strengthens bonds, and just plain makes us feel better. Even better, the Bible tells us it's a good thing. Some people think being a serious Christian means always looking like someone just egged their house. But Christians should be the happiest people on earth; we have the most to look forward to.

Your kids make you laugh. But do they *see* you laugh? The Bible tells us there's a time to laugh, that sharing joy lightens our load, and that laughing at ourselves relieves tension. Jesus may even have cracked a joke when He spoke of it being easier for camels to go through the eyes of needles than for rich people to get to heaven.

Laughter is especially important coming from you as a father. While God made you the bottom line for big decisions, He also wants you to reflect every part of His character—and that includes rejoicing over blessings and enjoying life.

A cheerful heart is good medicine.
PROVERBS 17:22 NLT

FEATS OF STRENGTH

Children can forgive their parents for being wrong,
but weakness sends them elsewhere for strength.
LEONTINE YOUNG

We men most often think of strength in terms of physical prowess or mental resolve, but that's not the most important type of strength for a dad. While that kind of strength says, "I can protect my family," it can also say, "I'm unapproachable."

When we meet pro athletes, they just seem so unlike us, so much more capable of doing great things than we are. They inspire us, but not in a way that affects what we do. It's when we see them out in the community, helping others, that we feel as if we can emulate them.

That's how it is for our kids. When they're little, it's fun for them to see you as the strongest man in the world because you can twirl them around or lift a bag of cement. But the kind of strength that really makes them feel secure can only be found in moments of tenderness—in bear hugs or in calm responses to big mistakes. Those moments are where true strength lies.

"Be strong, therefore, and prove yourself a man."
1 KINGS 2:2 NKJV

TRUE GRIT

*Bravery is the capacity to perform properly
even when scared half to death.*
OMAR BRADLEY

Your kids may think that being courageous means not being afraid. But after you turn on a nightlight, sit with them and let them in on something: everyone gets scared. Courage doesn't mean you're not afraid. It means you do what's right anyway. You trust that God is right there, even though you can't see Him. You believe that He cares about you and that He will always help you do the right thing.

Acting on the belief that God is with you no matter what still takes bravery, but not the kind that depends on you. From Moses appearing before Pharaoh to David taking up his sling to Jesus bearing His cross, the Bible is loaded with people who trusted God to have their backs. Make sure your kids know you have theirs, and let them know that no matter what, God is with all of you.

*Keep your eyes open, hold tight to your convictions,
give it all you've got, be resolute, and love without stopping.*
1 CORINTHIANS 16:13–14 MSG

GIVE TILL IT HURTS

I try to live my life like my father lives his. He always takes
care of everyone else first. He won't even start eating until
he's sure everyone else in the family has started eating.

BEN ROETHLISBERGER

Rare is the dad who wouldn't give his life to save one of his
children. As a father, however, you are actually required to
sacrifice something nearly as dear as your life—your free time.
Naps will be like luxury vacations, and you will seldom enjoy one
uninterrupted. Me-time in front of the TV will be replaced by
team-time, running to practices and games and performances
and appointments. You'll have to rethink what recharges you
and learn to fit it in whenever you can.

As you make these sacrifices, though, keep something in
mind: God sees every one of them, and when you do them out
of love, He will reward you with the satisfaction of seeing your
child well raised.

*Take your everyday, ordinary life—your sleeping, eating,
going-to-work, and walking-around life—and place it before
God as an offering. Embracing what God does for you
is the best thing you can do for him.*

ROMANS 12:1 MSG

SAFE AND SOUND

In Jesus Christ on the Cross there is refuge; there
is safety; there is shelter; and all the power of sin. . .
cannot reach us when we have taken shelter
under the Cross that atones for our sins.

A. C. DIXON

God promised the Israelites protection and provision in the
Promised Land, as well as rest from stress and despair when
they chose obedience to Him and His ways.

One of a father's most important jobs is to provide his family
security. There are physical, material ways to do that, but that's
not the limit of a dad's mandate. To make your family truly secure,
you need to make Jesus your own refuge. When there are no
fires to put out, do you still seek Him in prayer and in His Word?

Your family will have peace and rest when you show them
what resting in Jesus looks like, when you bring God into your
daily life and guide them in doing the same. When the going
gets hard, you'll be well practiced in the ways of God's peace
and security.

*"Then you would trust, because there is hope;
and you would look around and rest securely."*
JOB 11:18 NASB

SPIRITUAL LEADERSHIP

A man must talk to God about his children
before he talks to his children about God.
EDWIN LOUIS COLE

God has given you the responsibility for being your family's spiritual leader. What's the best way to do that? By going counterculture and moving back toward God and His truth. The Bible is full of God's designs and plans for you and your family. Every moment you spend in prayer and Bible study fills your tank and prepares you for whatever situations you face.

Look for the best example of spiritual leadership in Jesus Christ. Jesus didn't sit back and give orders. He was dropped straight down into the mix, into the dirt and blood of daily life, and He did so humbly and with appreciation for God and His ways. The result was that people followed Him because they wanted to, not because they had to. That's being a dad in a nutshell. When you set that kind of example, your kids won't be able to deny your integrity regarding God.

*Be diligent to present yourself approved to God
as a workman who does not need to be ashamed,
accurately handling the word of truth.*
2 TIMOTHY 2:15 NASB

TRANSMIT TRUTH

He that takes truth for his guide, and duty for his end,
may safely trust to God's providence to lead him aright.

BLAISE PASCAL

As a dad, you spend a surprising amount of time searching for truth. It starts simply, such as trying to sort out where that smell is coming from or who touched whom in the back of the car. The degree of difficulty increases during your children's adolescence, when you try to parse the meanings of such loaded statements as "No" and "I'm fine." A lot of that kind of detective work has to do with practical truth, but there's another category of truth undergirding it: personal truth.

That's why it's your job as a dad to demonstrate that only God's truth is truly personal. Not only does it provide a standard rooted in His unchangeable character, but it reveals something wonderful about God: He will guide and guard anyone who lives life based on what He says is true. That is comforting for both you and your kids, and it keeps them anchored amid cultural storms that threaten to drown them in lies.

My people, hear my teaching;
listen to the words of my mouth.
PSALM 78:1 NIV

KNOW YOUR REAL ENEMY

> I believe Satan exists for two reasons: first, the Bible
> says so, and second, I've done business with him.
> DWIGHT L. MOODY

In the middle of raising kids and dealing with one issue or conflict after another, it can be surprisingly easy to start viewing your kids as the enemy. There are a few things you need to remember in those unpleasant moments: one, it's normal to sometimes like least the people you love best, and two, you are not in fact each other's enemies.

Mankind's true enemy is not a toddler or a teen but a fallen angel who defied his maker, staged a coup, and got kicked to the curb. But because of Jesus, we know that God will not only deal with him at the right time but will help us overcome him in the meantime. Every other problem is caused by sin and the flesh, and Christ's blood cleanses us and the Holy Spirit guides us into godly living.

> *We are destroying speculations and every lofty thing*
> *raised up against the knowledge of God, and we are taking*
> *every thought captive to the obedience of Christ.*
> 2 CORINTHIANS 10:5 NASB

DADDY'S BOWLING WORDS

> You can preach a better sermon
> with your life than with your lips.
> OLIVER GOLDSMITH

Even when you're not aware of their presence, your kids are watching you. They see how you react when you get cut off driving out of the church parking lot, or when their mom burns dinner, or when they've disappointed you. And it all makes an impact.

We're all like containers, slowly filling up day by day with our thoughts, until they either overflow or we get bumped and they spill out. If you give anger and unforgiveness a foothold in your heart, that's what will flow over. And your kids will know that, for despite all your words about God and being good, your actions say anything goes when you're disappointed or hurt.

Make sure you are filling yourself up with God's words and that those words bear the fruit of God-pleasing deeds. That's how love and grace will flow from you into your kids' lives and, more importantly, their hearts.

> *He who looks into the perfect law of liberty and*
> *continues in it, and is not a forgetful hearer but a doer*
> *of the work, this one will be blessed in what he does.*
> JAMES 1:25 NKJV

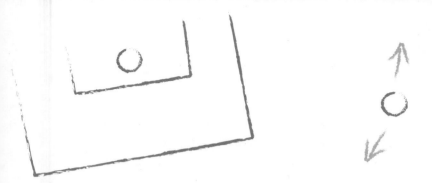

SESSION 1 PLAYBOOK:

Knowing and Following God

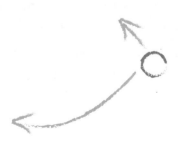

WHAT DO YOU LIVE FOR?

The deepest passion of the heart of Jesus was not the saving of men, but the glory of God; and then the saving of men, because that is for the glory of God.

G. CAMPBELL MORGAN

We all have a desire for meaning in our lives. But few understand that God made us for His glory and pleasure. Most think religion is for people whose guilt drives them to be good citizens.

Guilt actually has its purposes—such as driving us back to a God who wants to forgive us—but it shouldn't drive our lives. God isn't about religion but relationship. He has an abundant life for you, a life full of unexpected twists and turns and adventures, a life of the courageous exploration of swimming against the tide in simple, everyday ways.

Best of all, because God saved you to glorify Himself, you now operate under His authority and power. You are free from the world's expectations and constraints, anchored by His promises and His Spirit to Christ. There's nothing else worth living for.

LORD, you are my God; I will exalt you and praise your name, for in perfect faithfulness you have done wonderful things, things planned long ago.

ISAIAH 25:1 NIV

THE POWER OF THREE NAILS

*If you look up into His face and say, "Yes, Lord,
whatever it costs," at that moment He'll flood your
life with His provision and power.*

ALAN REDPATH

The Christian life is built on a blend of grace and obedience. It's not an either/or situation but a yes/and one. On one hand, grace is how you get saved. There's no way to God except through Jesus, and there's nothing you can do to earn His favor.

However, once you're on the road to heaven, you respond to God's grace by obeying Him. You don't obey Him so that you will be saved but because you already have been. It comes from a place of gratitude for what Jesus did on the cross, not from attempting to nail yourself to one.

The three nails that held Jesus to the cross are enough to rescue you from death's grasp, and the empty grave is enough to ensure that you can move through life in His power, filled with His Spirit and fueled by faith in all He has done.

*Like the Holy One who called you,
be holy yourselves also in all your behavior.*

1 PETER 1:15 NASB

REMEMBERING GOD

> We have a God who delights in impossibilities.
> BILLY SUNDAY

As a dad, you learn to appreciate why your own parents always seemed to forget stuff. Apparently forgetfulness turns out to be at least partly the by-product of having one or more messy, smelly, small people running around your house, creating a vortex of activity, yelling, and stickiness.

In those wonderfully busy moments, trying to remember God—to keep up in your relationship with Him—can slip out of your thoughts pretty quickly. But it's essential that you don't let that happen. More than that, it's a matter of obedience.

God first set aside the Sabbath as a day for the Israelites to stop working and take time for family and ponder His Word and ways. God deserves to be paused for and pondered, but He's also looking out for you. He knows that if you don't set aside a day to stop and smell the roses, life will swamp you. Be deliberate in taking time with your family to remember who God is and all He has done for you.

> I recall all you have done, O LORD;
> I remember your wonderful deeds of long ago.
> PSALM 77:11 NLT

TUNING IN

I f you don't set aside time to tune out from everything else and listen to God, life's noise will deafen you. But if you treat time with Him as a conversation, a back-and-forth conducted by the Holy Spirit, you'll learn to know when it's Him speaking—as opposed to your two-year-old hollering for more milk—or worse, Satan lying in your ear about what a lousy dad you are.

Carve out some time in a quiet place—during naps or soccer practice—and open up your Bible. Ask God to show you what He has for you in His Word. Ask questions and wait for His answer.

The better you know God from His Word, the more likely you'll be able to hear Him—in your heart, in scripture, in your kids, in a song, in the daily experiences that require you to stop and ask Him for advice.

If you wake me each morning with the sound of your loving voice, I'll go to sleep each night trusting in you. Point out the road I must travel; I'm all ears, all eyes before you.
PSALM 143:8 MSG

THERE'S KNOWING, AND THEN THERE'S KNOWING

There is no knowing that does not begin with knowing God.

JOHN CALVIN

We want to believe that God will work the way we think He should—instead of letting Him work the way He wants to. However, we can break this habit. When the Bible talks about knowing God, it means knowing Him more deeply—for who He says He is instead of what we think He is.

Parenting works similarly. We think we have a bead on one kid or the other—typical first child, typical boy, always resists change, never finishes chores—and rather than dig in and see what's really going on, we settle for that superficial level of knowledge about our children, rather than knowing what they're thinking at a given moment.

Just as you learn to ask God to help you know more of Him, you can also ask Him to help you know your kids more deeply. That's part of why Jesus came.

"This is eternal life, that they may know You, the only true God, and Jesus Christ whom You have sent."

JOHN 17:3 NASB

SEEKING THE HIGHEST GOOD

> Love is basic for the very survival of mankind. . . .
> He who hates does not know God. . . . Love is
> the supreme unifying principle of life.
> MARTIN LUTHER KING JR.

God's love took on hands and feet in Jesus, took on your greatest need—forgiveness—and did what was necessary to make a relationship with Him possible. He wants from you what you want from your kids: to love Him back.

But how do you love a God who is complete in and of Himself, who needs nothing from you, but who still wants you to love Him? Obedience is the short answer, but Jesus told you what that looks like: love God with everything you are, heart, soul, and mind.

He wants your passion and purpose, the best of your time, talent, and treasure, and the hardest, most pressing of your questions. He wants relationship. And when you strive for it, not only will you be satisfied, but His love will flow through you to your family.

> " 'You shall love the LORD your God with all your heart,
> with all your soul, and with all your mind.'
> This is the first and great commandment."
> MATTHEW 22:37–38 NKJV

STRATEGY SESSION 2:

RISK MANAGEMENT

THE RIGHT STUFF FOR THE HARD STUFF

It is not light we need, but fire; it is not the gentle
shower, but thunder. We need the storm,
the whirlwind, and the earthquake.

FREDERICK DOUGLASS

Sometimes, despite all your love and care for your kids, you not only don't get what you'd expected, but you get what you *never* expected—an illness or accident, an emotional crisis or trauma, a falling away from faith.

At times like those, it's natural to wonder where God is. But God's purposes are still in these hard times—perhaps more than in anything good or pleasant.

When Elijah hid out after his victory over the prophets of Baal, despairing for his life, there was a hurricane-force wind, an earthquake, and a great fire, but God wasn't in any of them. God came to His hurting and fearful prophet with a whisper, reminding Him that *in all things*, He is still God and He is still in control. Sometimes it takes a disaster to remind us of that, to test our resolve to trust Him in everything.

*"In this godless world you will continue to experience
difficulties. But take heart! I've conquered the world."*
JOHN 16:33 MSG

LIVING FREE

> Work like you don't need the money. Love like you've
> never been hurt. Dance like nobody's watching.
> SATCHEL PAIGE

To what are you completely committed? What things are unshakable for you? Your job, home, and health are all important, but your physical and financial circumstances can change overnight.

And be careful with principles too. It's a fine thing to commit to integrity and justice, but it's shockingly easy to make idols of these things. The same goes for your family. God has told you to be fruitful and multiply, to raise your children in His ways, and to love them sacrificially—but even they can slip into first place on your list when the sheer commitment it takes to be a dad overshadows God.

God should be your top priority, no ifs, ands, or buts. When you put pleasing Him first, you've committed to doing the best thing, and all those other good things fall into perspective. The freedom to love like Him comes when you learn to love Him best of all.

"May your hearts be fully committed to the LORD our God,
to live by his decrees and obey his commands, as at this time."
1 KINGS 8:61 NIV

YOU HAVE WHAT YOU NEED

We're often ashamed of asking for so much help because it
seems selfish or petty or narcissistic, but I think, if there's a
God—and I believe there is—that God is there
to help. That's what God's job is.

Anne Lamott

You probably remember when you received Jesus as Lord
and Savior, but do you recall your reaction when you first
learned that the Holy Spirit was now living in you, guiding you
and leading you into God's truth?

Let that soak in. God lives inside you. It's like He has put
a label on you that says, "This man is Mine, and My power is in
him." You also have the Bible, God's words and truth, recorded
for your benefit. God made the church for you too as His provision for relationships with like-minded people. Maybe your most
underused resource is prayer. You can talk to God and know that
He listens and responds. And finally, you have a mission in life:
sharing the Gospel and living by its power and light.

So when you wonder how you can possibly raise godly kids,
think of the answer in terms of the resources at your disposal.

Commit everything you do to the Lord.
Trust him, and he will help you.
Psalm 37:5 NLT

INFLUENCE = LEADERSHIP

You cannot antagonize and influence at the same time.
JOHN KNOX

The growing number of leadership books and consultants suggests a related issue: a growing need for authentic leadership, and the lack thereof.

Fortunately, you have Jesus as your example of the ultimate leader. As God, He alone could have played the boss card, demanding obedience and compliance from all. But instead, He played a different card: influence.

Despite all our shortcomings, God has made it clear that He wants a relationship with us. To prove it, He sent His best emissary, His Son, whose ministry was about helping, healing, and teaching, topped off with the sacrifice that made the relationship possible.

Jesus' example shows you all you need to be influential in your relationships, whether at work, at church, or at home. It's so simple but so effective: seek God's guidance, act humbly, make peace, pursue justice, and give and receive honest counsel. Being kind and calm in the face of adversity also wins hearts. This all goes into making you a leader worth following.

"Whoever wants to be a leader among you must be your servant, and whoever wants to be first among you must be the slave of everyone else."
MARK 10:43–44 NLT

GETTING THE HORSES
TO TAKE A DRINK

> God has no more precious gift to a church or an age than
> a man who lives as an embodiment of his will and inspires
> those around him with the faith of what grace can do.
>
> ANDREW MURRAY

Leadership is a question of attitude, not ability or qualification. If nothing else, you lead yourself, and if you're able to do that, you'll be able to lead others. It's that biblical principle of doing well with a little so that God can trust you with more.

Remember, leadership is all about influence, not bossing people around. Everything you do that promotes your children's highest possible good cultivates influence.

When you need to hold them accountable, they'll still be willing to go where you're headed. Your kids will know that you are for them, and when you direct them toward Jesus, because He's the One who influences you, you'll make a positive mark in their eternal landscape.

> *For I say, through the grace given to me, to everyone who*
> *is among you, not to think of himself more highly than he*
> *ought to think, but to think soberly, as God has*
> *dealt to each one a measure of faith.*
>
> ROMANS 12:3 NKJV

STAMP OF APPROVAL

*The Spirit of Christ. . .fills the Body, directs its movements,
controls its members, inspires its wisdom, supplies its
strength. He guides into truth, sanctifies its
agents, and empowers for witnessing.*
SAMUEL CHADWICK

If you think the world is going to hell in a handbasket, you're not wrong. If you think it may be harder than ever to raise godly kids, you may also be right. But so what? Has God changed? Is Jesus less in charge or the Spirit less present in you? No, no, and no.

God still has "all authority," and He has given it to you as His son and as a member of His body, the church. He made everything, and He has a role for you in His creation.

You are a leader, a hope bringer, a peacemaker, a light shiner, and a joy giver. Change begins with you embracing this reality, and it continues with your top-priority ministry as a dad.

*"Lord, I am not worthy to have you come into my home. Just say
the word from where you are, and my servant will be healed.
I know this because I am under the authority of my superior
officers, and I have authority over my soldiers."*
MATTHEW 8:8–9 NLT

STAY IN TOUCH

*Our love to God is measured by our everyday fellowship
with others and the love it displays.*
ANDREW MURRAY

Paul wrote that in encouraging others in the faith, we should "not neglect our meeting together, as some people do, but encourage one another" (Hebrews 10:25 NLT).

God's plan to glorify Jesus involves the fellowship of the church. It's part of His big picture of getting the Gospel out to the world. It's something only a group as large and diverse and spread out as the church could accomplish, and you get to be part of it.

Fellowship is also part of God's more personal picture for each Christian—getting us plugged in where we can learn and grow and help others do the same.

That translates to family too. God has a plan for each member of your family, but also a plan for you as a unit, all designed for your benefit and His glory. Making your kids a real part of church or small-group gatherings brings them into that ministry.

*But if we walk in the Light as He Himself is in the Light,
we have fellowship with one another, and the blood
of Jesus His Son cleanses us from all sin.*
1 JOHN 1:7 NASB

NO LOOKING BACK

The objects of the present life fill the human eye with a false magnification because of their immediacy.

WILLIAM WILBERFORCE

When setting priorities, ask yourself, *What lines up best with what I know to be true about God's priorities?* Jesus gave a few examples of this when some folks rejected His invitation to become His disciple, and He told them that anyone who put anyone ahead of Him had no place in the kingdom of God (Luke 9:57–62). Jesus wasn't saying it's bad to have a home or to bury your loved ones. . .unless you're just trying to put off following Him with all you have and are.

To determine God's priorities, you have to put Him first. Then you have to figure out whether what you're doing is your will or God's will. If you're putting God's kingdom first—which is relational in character and driven by His ultimate glory—you'll be able to see what you should do more clearly. Go for it, and trust God to honor those who honor Him.

Jesus said unto him, No man, having put his hand to the plough, and looking back, is fit for the kingdom of God.
LUKE 9:62 KJV

DRAIN THE TIME SINK

When you kill time, remember that it has no resurrection.
A. W. Tozer

A time sink is something that takes up your time with no real benefit, other than putting off something you'd rather not be doing. It's a new phrase for an old concept, one that goes back to when Adam procrastinated in telling the serpent to buzz off and leave his wife alone.

Today opportunities abound more than ever for putting off what you need to be doing. There are always emails to read, a game to finish, an app to check. It's one thing to take a break to recharge after a busy day; it's another to get sucked into your phone when you should be working, or playing video games when your wife needs help with dinner or the kids can't figure out their science fair project.

The stuff you need to do isn't nearly as fun as the stuff you want to do. Don't cut yourself off from fun, but remember what you've told your kids at the table: dessert only comes first on your birthday.

Teach us to number our days,
that we may gain a heart of wisdom.
Psalm 90:12 NKJV

STRESSED OUT? LOOK UP!

An hour of anxiety cannot change my circumstances,
but a minute of prayer can alter everything.

AL BRYANT

Fatherhood is awesome, but let's face it: parenting can be stressful. So how can God help? The answers may seem obvious, but they are tried and true.

First of all, pray. You can talk to God about what's going on, but then you can shift your attention from the day's craziness to God's worthiness to be praised. Worship is another way to let it go. Put on music that puts you in mind of your God. Sing along or just soak it in; it's hard to stay frazzled when you worship God.

Also, it's okay to ask for help. Ask God by all means, but then get over the tattered remnants of your ego and ask family, friends, or coworkers. Avoiding isolation works wonders because it short-circuits one of Satan's greatest hits: "You're the Only Fool Going through This." Remember, God doesn't give us worry and anxiety; He takes them away. Reading His Word is a good reminder of that.

Let patience have its perfect work, that you may
be perfect and complete, lacking nothing.

JAMES 1:4 NKJV

THE END OF YOURSELF

There are times when we must sink to the bottom of our
misery to understand truth, just as we must descend to the
bottom of a well to see the stars in broad daylight.

Vaclav Havel

Sometimes life does a dog pile on you. It happens to every
parent, so the mess itself is just life on earth. The concern
is how you respond. If you can't move past the exhaustion, and
it starts to turn into bitterness or outbursts of anger, those are
red flags. You should definitely ask for help, whether personal
or professional, to move you through it. But there's a spiritual
possibility for your downheartedness: you've been operating in
your own strength.

It's hard to recognize when you've shifted from God's sov-
ereignty in your life to an attempted coup on your own part. It's
often disguised as self-sufficiency, which is really your attempt
to assert independence from God. If you try to assert it long
enough, He'll give it to you—if only so you can see Him more
clearly through the dust and debris of your failure.

He gives power to the weak, and to those who
have no might He increases strength.
Isaiah 40:29 nkjv

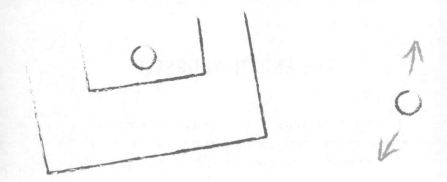

SESSION 2 PLAYBOOK:

Spiritual Risk Assessment

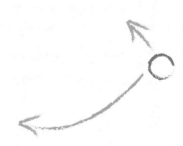

HOPE IS NOT A STRATEGY

Our goals can only be reached through a vehicle of a plan
in which we must fervently believe, and upon which we
must vigorously act. There is no other route to success.
PABLO PICASSO

Having kids complicates things in ways you never could have
imagined before they came along, and, as more than one
coach has told his team, "Failing to prepare is preparing to fail."

Making improvements in your daily decisions doesn't happen accidentally, and just hoping things work out doesn't help
either. Hope is not a strategy. Think through what you want to
accomplish and then plan. Don't overcomplicate the plan—and
resist perfectionist tendencies because they can paralyze you.

Think of one laser-focused action you can take. If family
time is a priority, start with one hour one night a week. If quiet
time is a priority, set aside fifteen minutes on weekdays. Make
it simple and doable. The goal is to know Jesus well enough to
rest in Him and follow His leading.

*"Is there anyone here who, planning to build a new house,
doesn't first sit down and figure the cost so
you'll know if you can complete it?"*
LUKE 14:28–29 MSG

FINDING YOUR STRENGTHS

We gain strength, and courage, and confidence by each experience in which we really stop to look fear in the face. . . . We must do that which we think we cannot.

<small>ELEANOR ROOSEVELT</small>

There's a voice inside you reminding you of your shortcomings. If you could read a transcript of the thoughts going through your mind daily, you'd be reading a bully's script—except you are both the bully and the victim. Learn to recognize this voice and silence it.

Human weakness opens the door for God's strength to shine. God has equipped you to fulfill your calling as a father, and He will continue to do so.

If you're not sure what your strengths are, ask someone you trust or take an assessment to get an idea. On one hand, be careful how you take what others say about you. On the other, trust the Bible: "By wise guidance you will wage war, and in abundance of counselors there is victory" (Proverbs 24:6 NASB).

May the God of peace. . .equip you with everything good for doing his will, and may he work in us what is pleasing to him, through Jesus Christ.

<small>HEBREWS 13:20–21 NIV</small>

NOTE YOUR ADVANTAGES

*Far and away the best prize that life offers is the
chance to work hard at work worth doing.*
THEODORE ROOSEVELT

God doesn't waste any of your experiences, good or bad. He delights in using them beyond what you thought possible. He can redeem your mistakes and elevate your accomplishments. You know God is at work when it's not possible for you to take all the glory.

What lens do you view life through? Is it the lens of self, where all your hustle and grind are about realizing your dreams? Is it comparison, where all your hard work is to make sure you're better off than you were growing up? Both can lead to impressive, though limited, accomplishments.

Your greatest advantage is that you belong to Jesus Christ. To belong to Him body, mind, and soul is the most liberating experience you can have. You are free from the world's expectations, free to enjoy work and family as part of your efforts to help build God's kingdom—the only endeavor that will last into eternity.

*Now all glory to God, who is able, through his mighty power
at work within us, to accomplish infinitely more
than we might ask or think.*
EPHESIANS 3:20 NLT

OPEN UP YOUR GIFTS

Do all the good you can. By all the means you can. In all the
ways you can. In all the places you can. At all the times you
can. To all the people you can. As long as ever you can.

JOHN WESLEY

Some people have a hard time believing they possess a gift-
ing, but others think they bring more to the table than they
actually do. God will usually anoint in private and confirm in
public—as He did with David. Likewise, there's no such thing
as secret gifts; all gifts are meant to bless the body of Christ.

No one sits on the bench on God's team, but not everyone
gets in the game either. Bench sitting is not God's game plan
but our refusal to see how we can be of service to His cause.
Once you commit to getting involved, the next step is to figure
out how.

Start by reading 1 Corinthians 12, where Paul breaks down
the possible roles individual believers can play. Then ask Him
what He wants you to do.

God has given each of you a gift from his great variety of
spiritual gifts. Use them well to serve one another.
1 PETER 4:10 NLT

GRATITUDE IS THE ATTITUDE

I would maintain that thanks are the highest form of thought,
and that gratitude is happiness doubled by wonder.
G. K. CHESTERTON

Gratitude starts with thinking about God, about who He is and what He has done for you. It can be as simple as admiring a sunset, a job well done, or anything that puts you in mind of God as the Creator.

Thinking of what Jesus went through to become your Savior should also be a source of constant thankfulness. No other religion features a God who died to save His followers, and no other god can match the intensity or faithfulness of our God's love and provision.

Being thankful can be more of a challenge when you don't feel like you have anything to be thankful for. Sometimes God's decisions disappoint you, even though you know His purposes include you. That's why the Bible talks about offering "a sacrifice of praise" (Hebrews 13:15 NIV)—because God deserves it even when you don't understand exactly why.

Through the LORD's mercies we are not consumed,
because His compassions fail not. They are new
every morning; great is Your faithfulness.
LAMENTATIONS 3:22–23 NKJV

GET CONNECTED

Fellowship means among other things that we are ready to
receive of Christ from others. Other believers minister
Christ to me, and I am ready to receive.

WATCHMAN NEE

When you hear the word *network*, you may think of business-
people who help each other get things done by making
connections, sharing experiences, and creating opportunities.
And then you may think, *That's fine, but I don't like networking. It
smacks of self-service and self-promotion, and that's not my bag.*
But the truth is, God made you to be part of a network; you are
made for relationship.

Some people are more relational than others. Some prefer
their personal space and are, for whatever reason, reluctant to
engage in friendships—lack of time, fear of rejection, anxiety
over being vulnerable. Regardless of how you're wired, fellowship is God's way of helping you mature through accountability,
encouragement, and admonishment.

What connections can you use for God's glory?

James, Peter, and John, who were known as pillars of the church,
recognized the gift God had given me, and they accepted
Barnabas and me as their co-workers. They encouraged us
to keep preaching to the Gentiles, while they
continued their work with the Jews.

GALATIANS 2:9 NLT

OWN YOUR DAD-NESS

A father should be his son's first hero
and his daughter's first love.
UNKNOWN

Some guys have wanted to be dads ever since they can remember, while others entered the club through the back door. Some grew into the idea, and others thought they had it all sorted out (at least up until they actually had kids; after that, any claims to perfection were strictly bravado). No matter how you entered the dad game, you are in it now, and it's up to you to make the most of it.

As a Christian, you are well aware that only God is perfect. Perfection shouldn't even be on the table as something to shoot for. Instead, just focus on getting better at it.

What traits make you a good dad? Ask three people who know you, care about you, and whose opinion you respect to give you three ways you are good as a dad and one way you could improve. Look for themes or patterns, and then pray about what God would have you do about what you've learned.

I have considered my ways and have
turned my steps to your statutes.
PSALM 119:59 NIV

DITCH THE PITY PARTY

*We either accept weaknesses in good people or
we have to tear pages out of the Bible.*
Robert Duvall

Facing the truth about yourself is key to the Christian life. You're keenly aware of your sin, and in some ways the consequences continue to ripple through your life. But you can be assured that in God's hands not one of your hardships or shortcomings is wasted. He either makes you stronger for having come through the storm, or He replaces your weakness with His strength.

It's one thing to ask someone to tell you your good qualities but much harder to ask him to tell you your bad ones. Remember that you're doing it to become a better man and father. When you have your responses, ask yourself if the weaknesses identified are negatively affecting your relationship with God or with those closest to you.

What are the long-term consequences if you don't do something about them now? Are you willing to live with them? If not, ask God if you need to take action, surrender, or have Him give you a different perspective.

*Fools think their own way is right,
but the wise listen to others.*
Proverbs 12:15 nlt

YOU'LL NEVER WALK ALONE

Whilst we deliberate how to begin a thing,
it grows too late to begin it.
QUINTILIAN

Fatherhood is a daunting job. Rarely does anyone go into it with complete confidence, and those who do soon find out that kids haven't read the same books they did and don't behave like they're supposed to. God, the perfect Father, has but one perfect child; the rest of us are works in progress.

Being a dad involves a lot of small actions that characterize the overall impact on a family. Don't waste time trying to control all of them. Leave it up to God to work things out for everyone's best interests.

That doesn't mean becoming passive. It's too easy to make excuses or quit trying, especially when you can't see the results of every seed you've planted (or every weed you've let grow too long). God isn't going to give up on you, so stick with Him.

"Who has made man's mouth? Or who makes the mute, the deaf,
the seeing, or the blind? Have not I, the LORD? Now therefore, go,
and I will be with your mouth and teach you what you shall say."
EXODUS 4:11–12 NKJV

GROWTH MIND-SET

We suffer primarily not from our vices or our weaknesses,
but from our illusions. We are haunted, not by reality,
but by those images we have put in their place.
DANIEL J. BOORSTIN

As a dad, you bear a lot of pressure. You're expected to deliver in multiple areas and with excellence. Financial pressures are some of the strongest fathers feel. Making a marriage work is right up there, followed by the high demands on your time and energy at home and work. And life seems designed to disarm you of the illusion of control over any of it.

Perfectionism is a harsh taskmaster. Holding on to the idea that life will be better "when. . ." or "as soon as we have. . ." is like chasing shadows. It drives you to lonely places and takes your energy away from being present with God and people.

What threatens your ability to be present with your family? If there's one thing the cross made clear, it's that you're not stuck with all your mistakes. In Christ there's always room to learn and grow—to develop a growth mind-set.

My God shall supply all your need according to
His riches in glory by Christ Jesus.
PHILIPPIANS 4:19 NKJV

KNOW YOURSELF TO LEAD YOURSELF

> Where I think the most work needs to be done
> is behind the camera, not in front of it.
> DENZEL WASHINGTON

What personality traits make being a dad hard for you? Some of them might serve you well at work but have the opposite effect at home. Do you talk to your kids in the same voice you use for serious meetings? Does your ability to spot potential problems at work make you stingy with praise at home?

Know yourself to lead yourself. Do you possess enough self-awareness to understand the impact of your behavior as you lead in different contexts (work, home, community)? You don't have to change who you are to change the actions you take.

If, for example, you are quick to spot problems, great! Use this trait in the right context. Beware that what works on the job may seem like harsh critique to your wife or children. Pray for perspective. Being aware of what it's like to be on the other side of you is key to making this effective.

> *Examine yourselves to see if your faith*
> *is genuine. Test yourselves.*
> 2 CORINTHIANS 13:5 NLT

DISCOVERING OPPORTUNITIES

We often miss opportunity because it's
dressed in overalls and looks like work.

Thomas Edison

One of the greatest proofs of God's choice to give people free will is in the massive buffet of choices we face each day. Some of them don't matter much—*Tea or coffee? Blue or striped socks?*—but others seem to carry the weight of the world—where to live, what job to take, what to do about the kids.

One of the reasons to look at your strengths and weaknesses is to figure out how to answer some of those harder questions. Sometimes the best choice is to do nothing or to wait until God's direction becomes clearer. Just be sure that when you ask Him for help, you take time to listen—and when He offers you a path, take it, even if, like Abraham, you're going to a place you don't know.

Sometimes people are reluctant to step up outside of the home because they think they are signing up for a lifetime commitment. What if you set a limit to your involvement and see where it leads? Keep trusting God and working hard, and it'll come together.

Whenever we have the opportunity,
we should do good to everyone.
Galatians 6:10 nlt

SEE A NEED, MEET A NEED

*I think you need to be intentional at times about your
leadership—where you're eating lunch, who you're interacting
with, making guys feel like you're interested in what
they're doing. If it's authentic, then it's going to be
an easy conversation and easy hangout time.*
AARON RODGERS

Marketing companies spend huge sums of money looking to
find perceived needs in the marketplace and then filling
them. Money-wise, it's worked out pretty well for some of them.
But as a Christian and a leader, you should have a different take
on meeting needs.

God has actually prepared tasks for which you are the perfect
person to get them done. Look at your life. What do you see? Is
there a need no one is filling that you can? Take God's point of
view on this. How can you please your Father in accomplishing
this task?

What a great model for your kids to follow when you talk to
them about your desire to please your own dad as well as God.

*We are His workmanship, created in Christ Jesus for
good works, which God prepared beforehand
that we should walk in them.*
EPHESIANS 2:10 NKJV

THREAT ANALYSIS AND RESPONSE

A godly leader. . .finds strength by realizing his weakness,
finds authority by being under authority, finds direction by
laying down his plans, finds vision by seeing the needs of
others, finds credibility by being an example, finds loyalty by
expressing compassion, finds honor by being faithful,
finds greatness by being a servant.

ROY LESSIN

Threats are double-edged swords. They can be things you avoid
or subjects you deal with head-on with God's perspective.

How do you deal with the obstacles you face in life? Many
things threaten a family—internet use/misuse, drugs, pornography, negative influences, ungodly worldviews. A lack of emotional
awareness can alienate you from your loved ones, and bad habits
(along with their secrets) damage trust.

Do you abdicate your leadership in these areas because
they're difficult to deal with and you don't have all the answers?
Talk to people who have had success in the areas you're concerned about, seek out resources, and above all pray for wisdom.
Do anything but give up.

*If anyone does not know how to manage his own family,
how can he take care of God's church?*
1 TIMOTHY 3:5 NIV

COMING UP SHORT

The acknowledgment of our weakness is
the first step in repairing our loss.
THOMAS À KEMPIS

Parenting has a way of humbling you like nothing else. It's one of the ways God teaches you patience. Because you cannot control all circumstances and outcomes, you have to reach out for help. The smart man looks to God. His long-term view of your life is to produce patience in you as part of His perfecting work.

When it comes to what matters most—your salvation, then growing in Christ and learning to be like Him in love and truth, words and deeds—your strengths only hold you back. It's like when Paul said that his impressive Jewish pedigree was all rubbish to him compared to knowing Jesus (Philippians 3:8).

Weakness can also lead you to accept that you have neither the strength nor the wisdom to make a move, which renders you completely dependent. That is the best place to be in relation to God.

The Holy Spirit helps us in our weakness. For example, we don't know what God wants us to pray for. But the Holy Spirit prays for us with groanings that cannot be expressed in words.
ROMANS 8:26 NLT

STRATEGY SESSION 3:

INJURY PREVENTION

WANTING ONLY GOD'S BEST

Love is not just a sentiment. Love is a great controlling
passion, and it always expresses itself in terms of obedience.
MARTYN LLOYD-JONES

You'd probably be pretty pleased if your kids turned out
smart, successful, and happy—but is that enough? It begs
the question, what are God's priorities for your kids? His Word
makes it clear: He wants His children to be holy and obedient.
That sounds pretty dry and joyless, but that's because those
words are typically associated with old-time saints, monks, and
martyrs. But think about the benefits of giving your life to Jesus.
He offers abundant life now and eternal life in the future. There's
adventure in that—but we have to be different than those in the
world. We must be holy, set apart for God's purposes and glory.

God is anti-sin but not anti-happiness. In fact, pursuing
holiness is one of the keys to happiness. True holiness means
understanding that Jesus is the source of happiness. If you
want the things He wants, the other things competing for your
attention will lose their shine.

"May your loyal servants rejoice in your goodness."
2 CHRONICLES 6:41 NLT

EFFORT, NOT PERFECTION

If human beings are perceived as potentials rather than
problems, as possessing strengths instead of weaknesses,
as unlimited rather than dull and unresponsive,
then they thrive and grow to their capabilities.

BARBARA BUSH

When an expectation isn't met, conflict results, expressed in anger, sadness, anxiety, or even shame. We get upset about expectations we didn't realize we had until they went unmet. Teenagers seem to be in this state constantly, but younger kids feel it too, and they struggle to express what they're feeling.

Most of the time we assume others know what we expect, so we have to get better at expressing our expectations. Discuss expectations with your kids, especially as they get a bit older and want an allowance or a phone or a car. Ask them what they expect, and share what you expect. Then you can talk about what's realistic and unrealistic. Negotiate wisely. The idea isn't to lower expectations but to make them achievable.

The scenario may be complex, but the key to managing expectations is comparatively simple: praise effort, not ability.

*Make me truly happy by agreeing wholeheartedly with
each other, loving one another, and working
together with one mind and purpose.*
PHILIPPIANS 2:2 NLT

STAY ON THE SUNNY SIDE

We know the excitement of getting a present—we love to
unwrap it to see what is inside. So it is with our children;
they are gifts we unwrap for years as we discover
the unique characters God has made them.

Cornelius Plantinga

Keeping hope alive is essential to being a parent. The best kind
of hope doesn't come from being popular or a good student.
Success comes and goes, and defeat is often a better teacher.
But God's love in Christ doesn't change. It's the one thing you
can count on through all of life's ups and downs. Nothing can
separate you from Christ's love. His love sustains hope.

Hope in Jesus matters more than financial security, more
than health, more than the passing fancies we call happiness.
As you coach your children through life, make sure they know
all the good qualities you see in them. They need to hear about
the joy you have in them—not because of their potential but
because they exist.

*For in hope we have been saved, but hope that is seen is
not hope; for who hopes for what he already sees?*

Romans 8:24 nasb

GET WISE

Where there is charity and wisdom,
there is neither fear nor ignorance.
Francis of Assisi

T o teach your kids the value of wisdom is to give them a firm foundation on which all other principles can be constructed. The Bible has a lot to say about teaching wisdom to kids; just going through the book of Proverbs on a regular basis will help you understand the value of wisdom and how to apply it to their lives.

Once you've made a habit of preparing yourself to be wise, you can effectively teach your children about wisdom's importance. Godly wisdom contrasts with worldly wisdom, such as the kinds of things your kids will hear from well-meaning unbelievers, like "Always follow your heart." Contrast that with what the Bible says: "The heart is deceitful above all things and beyond cure. Who can understand it?" (Jeremiah 17:9 NIV).

Wisdom teaches that your children's identity is in Christ, not in feelings, fashion, or fads. When they store it in their hearts, your kids will be able to go out in the world with confidence.

Keep vigilant watch over your heart;
that's where life starts.
Proverbs 4:23 msg

WHY IT'S IMPORTANT TO
REALLY CHEW

> Beaver: Gee, there's something wrong with just
> about everything, isn't there, Dad?
> Ward: Pretty much, Beav.
> *LEAVE IT TO BEAVER*

With boundaries established, you can have fun with your kids around tech. When your kids crack jokes or make inside references, ask where they heard or saw them. Do it with interest, not accusation; think of it as research, not inquisition. If you have concerns, let them know. If you don't, let them know that too. Play their games with them; watch their shows and listen to their music—they will love that you are interested in what means so much to them.

Showing such interest will provide opportunities to discuss what concerns your kids—what they like, subtle agendas and messages, what the Bible says about the issues in play. Teach them that they should always be asking, *What does God think about this?*

When you demonstrate that God wants both their hearts and minds engaged with Him, you're planting seeds of responsible thinking and helping them see the value of processing what they see and hear from a biblical perspective.

*Solid food is for those who are mature, who through training have
the skill to recognize the difference between right and wrong.*
HEBREWS 5:14 NLT

FACE-TO-FACE

Electric communication will never be a substitute for the
face of someone who with their soul encourages
another person to be brave and true.

CHARLES DICKENS

Until we are face-to-face with God, we'll only know other people and ourselves imperfectly, as Paul said, "like puzzling reflections in a mirror" (1 Corinthians 13:12 NLT). In the meantime, we strive for better communication—with God in prayer, with ourselves in reflection, and with our kids on a daily basis.

While technology has made communication easier than ever, it has also created more distance between people. Texting is quick and easy, and social media allows us to keep up with friends and family. But community is more than constant information. It's about really getting to know others.

One day you will see God face-to-face; you will know Him and be known by Him. That day will be amazing. You can have a taste of that now, through getting to know another person's thoughts, fears and joys, plans, and problems. When you come to truly know someone, you value that person more highly.

"What a relief to see your friendly smile.
It is like seeing the face of God!"
GENESIS 33:10 NLT

BULLIES

Never do a wrong thing to make a friend—or to keep one.
ROBERT E. LEE

Bullying is one of the great nightmares of this age of information. The anonymity of the cyber age is tailor-made for blasting others for all the reasons that make a bully a bully: displaying power over others, lashing out in pain or insecurity, trying to fit in, or just exercising a mean streak.

Bullying is a complex issue, but one that, as a dad, you can't ignore. Be ready to talk about it, because your kids are likely to deal with it at some point. Gauge their feelings before you respond. Make sure they understand that bullying is never okay—because it's not okay with God.

Talk about why kids bully, what to do about bullying, and if it's happened to them; be available and partner with them. Every time they go online or encounter someone, your kids have the chance to make the world a better place by being kind, considerate, respectful, and caring.

I will call upon the LORD, who is worthy to be praised;
so shall I be saved from my enemies.
PSALM 18:3 NKJV

THE BLACK DOG

Anxiety does not empty tomorrow of its sorrows,
but only empties today of its strength.
CHARLES H. SPURGEON

Winston Churchill famously referred to his depression as a "black dog" that sat in his lap regularly. Though at times the great preacher Charles Spurgeon's depression weakened him to the point of wanting to die, he felt that God had purposes in it—including making him more compassionate.

Depression seems like a pet many kids bring home. It's necessary to send them a crucial message: it's okay to get help. Though there is no shame in seeking counseling and even medication if the sadness, loneliness, or anger continues over time, it's a good idea to try some homemade remedies first. Encourage regular exercise and healthy eating, regular hydration, and lots of sleep. If something big has happened in a child's life, don't let it go undiscussed.

Overcoming depression can be a trial-and-error process, so keep calm and seek God for your child's help, hope, and comfort.

" 'I've picked you. I haven't dropped you.' Don't panic.
I'm with you. There's no need to fear for I'm your God.
I'll give you strength. I'll help you. I'll hold you
steady, keep a firm grip on you."
ISAIAH 41:10 MSG

KEEP YOUR HEAD ON A SWIVEL

Suicide is a permanent solution to a temporary problem.
PHIL DONAHUE

S uicide always strikes like a thief in the night, leaving broken
hearts and unanswerable questions. Your child will deal with it
in some way, either because she has had those thoughts herself
or because she knows someone who has.

Suicide makes headlines and provides a subject for TV shows,
none of which do a struggling kid any favors in shedding light
or hope. "Just kill yourself" is a social media tagline, a throw-
away line that does nothing to stop a kid who's thinking about
throwing away his life.

Look for signs: self-harm, smoking, shoplifting, eating disor-
ders, alcohol or drug use. If you see signs, engage. Low impulse
control is a developmental problem for teens. Spend time gently
probing, remembering they may be feeling shame or rejection.
Don't compound it. Jesus didn't shame sinners.

The Bible is full of people who dealt with dark days—and
lifted them up to God. Lead your kids in seeking His comfort.

*Why am I discouraged? Why is my heart so sad? I will put my
hope in God! I will praise him again—my Savior and my God!*
PSALM 42:11 NLT

WANT THE WEATHER TO CHANGE?
WAIT FIVE MINUTES

It takes courage to grow up and
become who you really are.
E. E. CUMMINGS

The best thing you can tell your kids about puberty is that it's survivable. You are living proof. A lot of dealing with it is commiserating when you can. As Carol Burnett once said, "Adolescence is just one big walking pimple."

With all the big changes, a bit of disconnection is standard. The kid you thought you understood pretty well suddenly becomes inscrutable, which can be annoying. But don't freak out or check out! Give it your best shot. Go for a walk; ask what happened and how he's feeling.

Ongoing deterioration in behavior means you're probably going to have to get some outside help, but sometimes kids just need time and space to process. With boys, watch for withdrawal, anger, and aggression. With girls, watch for tears and being more verbose when asked what's wrong.

Be content with who you are, and don't put on airs.
God's strong hand is on you; he'll promote you at the right
time. Live carefree before God; he is most careful with you.
1 PETER 5:6–7 MSG

HOW TO LOVE YOUR LITTLE TYRANT

> Before I got married I had six theories about bringing up
> children, and now I have six children and no theories.
> JOHN WILMOT, EARL OF ROCHESTER

Toddlers are a blast, but under all the fun times and sweet moments there lurks a tiny dictator. It's human nature, but with some kids, it's also the result of a strong will looking to assert dominion over all it surveys. What's a biblical response? Swift, decisive spankings to make it clear who's boss? Or a "Come, let us reason together" approach?

Maybe both. But either way, your best move is to pray. A lot. Teach your kids Colossians 3:20: "Children, always obey your parents, for this pleases the Lord" (NLT). And teach yourself 1 Thessalonians 5:17: "Pray without ceasing" (NKJV).

Curiosity and exploration should be encouraged, but you also need to enforce what you instruct your child to do to keep that child safe. Stay on your little one's team, even when it seems like you're losing. God is faithful. He made your child to be an explorer—that's how kids learn—so no guilt is required from you. But set boundaries, and give God time to work out His purposes.

> *Point your kids in the right direction—*
> *when they're old they won't be lost.*
> PROVERBS 22:6 MSG

HAVE A HEART

Wicked men obey from fear; good men, from love.
AUGUSTINE

What do you picture when you close your eyes and think of your kids? Do you try to catch them being good, or do you see only the bad? Your kids aren't molded only by your interactions with them; they are also shaped by perception—how they see a situation or hear a comment, regardless of your intent or the context. You can't possibly know everything they are experiencing or thinking, especially as they get older. But God knows all of it.

How does God operate with you, knowing as He does all of your feelings and thoughts? With grace. His heart is always geared toward your highest good, because the more you cooperate with Him to become like Jesus, the greater His glory.

Rather than feeling overwhelmed at everything you wish you'd done better, trust that God is faithful to work in and around your child just as He has with you. Have hope for your child; remind him of his value and your love, especially when it gets tough.

Always be humble and gentle. Be patient with each other,
making allowance for each other's faults because of your love.
EPHESIANS 4:2 NLT

WHY SO ANGRY?

It is understanding that gives us an ability to have peace.
When we understand the other fellow's viewpoint,
and he understands ours, then we can sit
down and work out our differences.

HARRY S. TRUMAN

Anger isn't necessarily a sin; how you handle it can be. Remember, you are a new creation in Christ, and your old ways of handling disappointment or frustration died on the cross.

When your kids get angry, are they displaying immaturity, or do they have a legitimate reason? Are you the cause? Are you keeping promises, making them feel wanted, giving them appropriate autonomy? Or are you inadvertently manipulating or ignoring them? Look inward and then ask God for insight.

Kids aren't always able to clearly express their feelings. Teach them to calm down, then give them a voice and listen. Uncover the issue at the heart of the anger. Find ways to bleed off the anger and then channel it, but make sure you follow up with a sit-down, talk, and prayer. Everyone loses in a power struggle.

Lead with your ears, follow up with your tongue, and let anger straggle along in the rear. God's righteousness doesn't grow from human anger.

JAMES 1:19–20 MSG

BREATHE IN, BREATHE OUT

Don't fear the future. God is already there.
BILLY GRAHAM

Nonstop demands are part of being a parent. There is always something to do, whether it's an appointment, chore, or crisis. Manageable stress can quickly shift into full-blown anxiety, especially because, as a dad, your imagination always goes to the worst-case scenario. A bad grade becomes a future living under a bridge; a dislike of broccoli becomes a lifetime of cheese puffs and soda.

It's as though becoming a dad activates some previously hidden catastrophe gene. But estimates indicate that 98 percent of what people worry about never happens. And most of the other 2 percent is survivable.

God wants to step in and give you peace—not *calm*, mind you, but assurance that there's a way through all the busyness. You have to follow His orders, though, and that means praying as often as you think of something that needs prayer. It means turning your attention to others, but it also means carving out time to recharge. And remember to *breathe.*

"Do not be afraid or discouraged, for the LORD will
personally go ahead of you. He will be with
you; he will neither fail you nor abandon you."
DEUTERONOMY 31:8 NLT

BURNOUT

Burnout is what happens when you try to
avoid being human for too long.
MICHAEL GUNGOR

Remember the psalm about thirsting for God like a deer panting for water (Psalm 42)? Picture this deer, running hard. He narrowly escapes a wolf, but he finds himself out where the trees turn into desert. The fear is bleeding off, and he's exhausted. He is desperate to quench his thirst. He can't be proactive; he's just trying not to collapse and die.

This buck is tired of putting out one fire after another, helping with algebra homework, transporting Bambi to baseball practice and piano practice and swim practice and counseling. He is burnt out. What can he do?

First, he can get away and recharge. Then he should declutter his life, prioritizing only what absolutely needs to be done and taking a break from everything else. That will create mental space so he can seek God and listen. Replenishing your soul is not a luxury but a necessity.

*Then, because so many people were coming and going that
they did not even have a chance to eat, [Jesus] said to them,
"Come with me by yourselves to a quiet place and get some rest."*
MARK 6:31 NIV

THINGS UNSEEN

Faith is not belief without proof,
but trust without reservation.
ELTON TRUEBLOOD

Faith is belief in God and His promises and commands. Jesus said some have great faith and others have little. He healed or helped the ones who had great faith and admonished those who didn't. So faith seems to come in degrees.

Trusting in what you don't see can be hard. Do you really believe that God knows best and is concerned about you becoming more like Jesus? Is the God you're trusting the One who spoke the earth into creation and told the wind and waves to chill, or is He some version you've manufactured, one limited by your limiting thoughts of Him?

Ask God for more faith—and expect Him to give you opportunities to put it into practice. Learn His Word and promises, and obey Him. When you put your faith into action, the reality of God blooms into peace and confidence, a generous, never-ending source of life.

The fundamental fact of existence is that this trust in God,
this faith, is the firm foundation under everything that makes
life worth living. It's our handle on what we can't see.
HEBREWS 11:1 MSG

READY FOR THE FRONT LINES

Fellowship with God means warfare with the world.
CHARLES E. FULLER

Never underestimate the reality of spiritual warfare. When you try to do something God's way, you in effect paint a target on your back. The devil will do all he can to discourage or neutralize the threat of a man committed to raising his kids for God's glory. Don't be shocked when things suddenly take a turn—especially when they've been going well lately.

God allows Satan to mess with you because it's His way of testing you to make you stronger so you'll be prepared for what comes next. Jesus said you could count on the world hating you, but He also said He would be with you all the way. That promise goes for your kids too.

Once you grasp the battle at hand, prepare for it. Meet with other Christian men for Bible study and support. Learn to defend your faith—to win souls, not arguments.

You must worship Christ as Lord of your life. And if someone asks about your hope as a believer, always be ready to explain it.
1 PETER 3:15 NLT

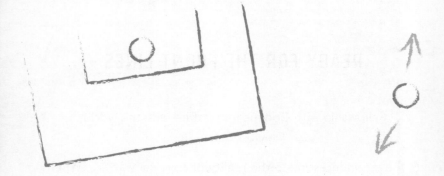

SESSION 3 PLAYBOOK:

God's Promises

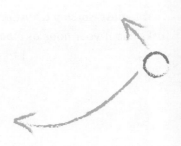

YOUR LIFE'S ANCHOR

I believe the promises of God enough
to venture an eternity on them.
ISAAC WATTS

Do you want good things for your kids? Do you want to take care of their basic needs? Do you want to help them become the best people they can be, to encourage and support the best use of their time and talents, to see them enjoying fruitful relationships with good people? Of course you do.

God has promised those same things to you as His son. How do you think He feels when you respond, "Thanks, but I'm going to try it my way"? Didn't He get enough of that from the Israelites in the wilderness?

Is God's Word enough for you to take Him up on His promises? If you ever need something reliable, life-changing, strengthening, rest-giving, helpful, wise, protecting, providing, comforting, hopeful, or joyous, take a look at God's promises. Then take them to heart. They're for you.

*"Come to Me, all you who labor and are heavy laden,
and I will give you rest. Take My yoke upon you and learn
from Me. . .and you will find rest for your souls."*
MATTHEW 11:28–29 NKJV

SAFE PASSAGE

If the Lord be with us, we have no cause of fear. His eye is
upon us, His arm over us, His ear open to our prayer—
His grace sufficient, His promise unchangeable.

JOHN NEWTON

This world is broken. It wasn't when God made it, but sin quickly changed that. Sin not only executed the human spirit but washed over creation like a tsunami. Beauty and goodness can still be found in this world, but you have to look for it. The first thing that catches the eye is all the trouble mankind has caused. As a dad, one of your biggest concerns is, *How do I get my kids through this safely?*

The Bible contains literally thousands of God's promises. But while many verses speak of His peace and rest, none guarantee a smooth ride through life. That would be nice, but would it be for the best?

Instead, God's promises are for safe passage. The journey you're on, through all the valleys and shadows of this world, is covered under His protection and provision.

God is our refuge and strength,
an ever-present help in trouble.

PSALM 46:1 NIV

FINISH THE JOB

The work of grace is but begun in this life; it is not finished
here; as long as we are in this imperfect state,
there is something more to be done.

MATTHEW HENRY

You know the importance of finishing what you start, and so does God. However, it's important to keep in mind that a job well done isn't one in which nothing unexpected or detrimental happens. But God uses all of that, building bridges out of broken parts and making straight paths out of crooked sticks.

You'll still carry the scars from accidents and mistakes and injuries, especially ones of your own making. You'll bear the pain of watching your kids struggle with the same basic challenges of being imperfect humans in need of forgiveness and salvation. But God will bring to completion everything He started in your life and theirs.

Life's setbacks vary in size, but they're all possible to overcome because God is with you.

*I am confident of this very thing, that He who began a good
work in you will perfect it until the day of Christ Jesus.*
PHILIPPIANS 1:6 NASB

JUST ASK ALREADY!

As long as I have God's Word, I know that I am walking in
His way and that I shall not fall into any error or delusion.

MARTIN LUTHER

Nothing can truly prepare you for fatherhood except being a
dad. You may have had a great dad as an example, so you'll
know what you're shooting for. Or your dad might have been a
louse or just not there, so you'll know what to avoid.

You may have read dozens of books on godly parenting and
have a master's degree in child psychology, and while that kind
of preparation is useful, you just don't know what you don't
know. You just know you love the little stinkers—and that's a
great place to start.

God promises that what you lack in wisdom, He will give
you, generously and without guilt trips, if you just ask. Those
head-scratching moments are your cue to take a step back and
seek the wisdom of the only Father who ever had it all sorted
out before His kids were born.

*If any of you lacks wisdom, let him ask of God, who gives to all
liberally and without reproach, and it will be given to him.*

JAMES 1:5 NKJV

GOD'S GOT YOUR SIX

I will not fear, for you are ever with me, and you will
never leave me to face my perils alone.

Thomas Merton

J ust when you think you're starting to get the hang of parenting, something blindsides you. You'll beat yourself up over it,
whether it's small or big, because that's what dads do. But you
need to remind yourself that God is a God of grace and mercy
and forgiveness, and best of all, a God of wisdom.

After all, God is the ultimate parent. He brought all life
into being and established relationships and boundaries and
rules for better living. He understands the value of natural
consequences, but He is always willing to forgive and forget.
Why wouldn't you ask Him for help with your kids?

Since God wants the same thing you do—to see your kids
grow up into the amazing people He made them to be—make a
habit of asking Him what to do. He has your back.

Be content with such things as you have. For He Himself
has said, "I will never leave you nor forsake you."
Hebrews 13:5 NKJV

PEACE OF MIND

The future is as bright as the promises of God.
WILLIAM CAREY

The New Testament Greek word for "worry" means "to divide your mind," and the root of the English word means "to strangle or choke." It's clear that worry is not good for mind or body. And yet opportunities to worry constantly present themselves. If you want to obey God's command not to worry but you're still concerned about what's going on with your children, how can you keep your mind from being divided?

Start with God. Remember who you are as His son. Remember what Jesus said about lilies and sparrows (Matthew 6:26)? When you worry, you're saying you're not as valuable as God says you are. Furthermore, worry doesn't work (v. 27).

Let worry be a reminder to place things in God's care, trusting that He cares for you and your kids and that He will keep His promises to take care of your needs.

Don't fret or worry. Instead of worrying, pray. Let petitions and praises shape your worries into prayers, letting God know your concerns. Before you know it, a sense of God's wholeness, everything coming together for good, will come and settle you down.
PHILIPPIANS 4:6–7 MSG

WASH YOUR FEET

Forgiveness is the giving, and so the receiving, of life.
GEORGE MACDONALD

Our greatest need as humans is forgiveness. That's why God sent us a Savior instead of a teacher, scientist, economist, or entertainer. And with salvation, Jesus promises us both eternal life in heaven and abundant life now.

Jesus had to persuade his stubborn friend Peter to let Him wash his feet. When Jesus said, "Or else we're done," Peter shouted, "Lord, wash my hands and head too!" You can almost hear the smile in Jesus' response: "He who has bathed needs only to wash his feet, but is completely clean" (John 13:10 NASB).

It's as if Jesus was saying, "We're not talking about dirty feet, Pete. I meant that once I've cleansed you of sin, you can ask Me for forgiveness for the other everyday sorts of sins you'll still be committing until I come back." That's a promise to keep close by, and it's a reminder that once you belong to Jesus, nothing can separate you from His love.

If we confess our sins, he is faithful and just to forgive us our sins, and to cleanse us from all unrighteousness.
1 JOHN 1:9 KJV

PLANTED IN GOOD SOIL

Don't let what you cannot do interfere with what you can do.
JOHN WOODEN

When your kids are little, make sure they hear you speak God's words. When they get older, other voices will vie for their attention and hearts, so stick to your guns, even when the way they mimic the world's views discourages you. Trust God that His Word accomplishes His purposes. It worked for you, didn't it?

In the parable of the sower (Matthew 13:1–23), Jesus described four different responses to the Word of God. He depicted hearts as soil—some too hard; others too shallow; some thorny; and the best kind, the fertile and rich. Ask God to take your heart and the hearts of your children and turn them toward each other (Malachi 4:4–6), bridged by the promises in His Word.

Ultimately you won't be able to control your children's decision to follow Jesus—but with God's promises as your foundation, you can most certainly influence them in the right direction.

We will speak the truth in love, growing in every way more and more like Christ, who is the head of his body, the church.
EPHESIANS 4:15 NLT

HE WILL WORK IT OUT

Prayer is the promise utilized. A prayer which is not based
on a promise has no true foundation.

CHARLES H. SPURGEON

The tendency to catastrophize haunts every parent, but God
doesn't play that game. Paul wrote Romans 8 to tell believers
what it means to live according to God's promises. It boils down
to choosing between two ways of living: the flesh or the Spirit.
The flesh was your default, pre-Jesus setting, when the desire
to please yourself drove you.

But because the Holy Spirit lives in you, you have God's
promise that you are His. That means you belong to Him now,
not yourself, and the perks of adoption are outstanding: you can
live free from fear—both of death and hell but also of anything
that threatens you in this life.

The famous verse doesn't tell us "God works *some* things
together for good," or "Things work out for good every so often." "All things" means *all* things, so you're covered, and so is
your family.

We know that all things work together for good to them that love
God, to them who are the called according to his purpose.

ROMANS 8:28 KJV

STRATEGY SESSION 4:

EFFECTIVE COMMUNICATION

STICKS AND STONES

God is ready to assume full responsibility
for the life wholly yielded to Him.

ANDREW MURRAY

The power of a dad's words can't be underestimated. You have your hand on the button of your children's hearts, and your words are the key to making peace or bringing about emotional destruction. While it's true that actions speak louder than words, the way you use your words (or don't) is an action, just as is using your hands to build something.

Depending on the kinds of words you heard (or didn't hear) growing up, your default setting may be those words. That's fine if they're helpful but not if they tear down or discourage. A few well-placed words are like the key Jenga block—they'll either keep the structure standing when you avoid them or bring it all down if you don't.

God speaks most beautifully through words of kindness, encouragement, and healing. When is the last time you praised your child? Those simple, heartfelt moments can fortify your child for a lifetime.

I will instruct you and teach you in the way you should go;
I will counsel you with my loving eye on you.

PSALM 32:8 NIV

GOD IS IN THE DETAILS

*The difference between something good and
something great is attention to detail.*
CHUCK SWINDOLL

It's hard to listen to your kids—*really* listen to them, not just wait for key words that trigger your autopilot so you can interrupt and tell them what to do next. It's hard to know for sure what's a big deal and what isn't, so listening well is essential. Ask for God's wisdom as you do.

Be patient. What seems superficial to you may be vital to them. Feeding back the little details may help them move toward the heart of the matter. Saying "yes" and "uh-huh" and "I see" often will keep them talking and get you closer to the issue at hand.

Conversation should be a discovery process for both sides: you want to find out what's important to your kids, and you want them to hear their own arguments. You can label their feelings without validating them: "You sound hurt/angry/sad about that. It doesn't seem fair." When you uncover the truth, then you can bring godly wisdom to the situation.

*The eyes of the LORD are on the righteous,
and His ears are open to their cry.*
PSALM 34:15 NKJV

HOSTAGE NEGOTIATIONS

The most important thing in communication
is to hear what isn't being said.
PETER F. DRUCKER

Talking with your kids can feel like negotiating a hostage situation—and you're the one being held for ransom. Perhaps surprisingly, advanced techniques in hostage negotiations are not only required but reflect a biblical approach of empathy and truth seeking.

In truth the hostage is your child, caught up in an issue, overwhelmed by feelings, and needing you to show her the way through. It'll take her awhile to get to the point, so stay engaged, asking clarifying questions and getting her to tell a story that has a beginning, middle, and end.

Listening actively means trying to draw out your child's emotions and the voice in his head that is competing with yours. Don't interrupt or evaluate; just listen, affirming his points with nods or *yeses*, and ask open-ended questions (not answerable with a yes or no) to show you are paying attention.

Your kids may understand that you are on their side, but this kind of listening will demonstrate it.

The purposes of a person's heart are deep waters,
but one who has insight draws them out.
PROVERBS 20:5 NIV

TAKING NOTES

The simple act of paying attention can take you a long way.
KEANU REEVES

Being a good dad requires attention to detail. If you're a detail guy, that's right in your wheelhouse, but if you're more of a big-picture kind of thinker, then you're going to have to be deliberate about it. Picking up on the way your kids communicate can make all the difference when it comes to either getting your message across or receiving theirs.

When your kids talk, pay attention to both the how and the when. When are they more likely to speak in useful ways—before school, after school, not until fed? Are they more likely to speak at a slower pace, like a fire hose, or while not being questioned?

Then go with that time or style when you engage them. Find the best times, ways, and even places. Mind your tone. Remember the big picture: you're trying to tell them that you care about relationship, just like God does.

My goal is that they may be encouraged in heart and united in love, so that they may have the full riches of complete understanding, in order that they may know the mystery of God, namely, Christ.
COLOSSIANS 2:2 NIV

KEEP IT REAL

Pride makes us artificial and humility makes us real.
THOMAS MERTON

Communication is a two-way street, with messages being sent and received. But how you most effectively communicate is another question entirely. There's a balance between being the bottom line and being open and approachable. You want your kids to learn self-control, but you don't want to take away their curiosity or burgeoning independence.

Use small chunks of information. Engage them in a brief discussion centered on the pertinent facts and what their options are. Explain expectations and consequences without falling into nag mode. If they make themselves late for school, let them explain to their teachers. If you have to do their chores, dock their allowance.

God makes His expectations clear in His Word; it's a good model. Being steady, calm, and consistent will open the door for other conversations, both meaningful and fun. Your kids are actual people, so talk to them as you would any other actual person.

*I, too, try to please everyone in everything I do. I don't just
do what is best for me; I do what is best for
others so that many may be saved.*
1 CORINTHIANS 10:33 NLT

YOU MAKE A BETTER
WINDOW THAN A DOOR

Honesty and transparency make you vulnerable.
Be honest and transparent anyway.
MOTHER TERESA

Dads are uniquely powerful figures in their kids' lives. Maybe that's because we're like their first glimpse of what God is like. But the bottom line is, your kids care what you think.

Don't get caught up in how you think a dad is supposed to act. Just be yourself, holding the line when you have to, but being free with praise, support, and hugs. Letting your kids get to know the real you is a great gift.

Just as you ask your children to tell you about their days, you can tell them about yours too. And they love to hear stories about when you were their age—especially if you got in trouble! Such honesty and vulnerability open a window to letting them see how they might someday be as great as they think you are and how God must be as wonderful as you say He is.

We have depended on God's grace, not on our own human
wisdom. That is how we have conducted ourselves
before the world, and especially toward you.
2 CORINTHIANS 1:12 NLT

SETTING BOUNDARIES

*I'm never more courageous than when I'm embracing
imperfection, embracing vulnerabilities, and setting
boundaries with the people in my life.*
BRENÉ BROWN

When you've made a practice of being honest and open with your kids, you'll find it's actually easier to talk to them about harder things, like poor decisions they've made. Making your expectations simple and clear for them is important. Making them aware of the expectations they should have for you as a dad is also a good idea.

That's a deep concept, so save it till they're a little older. But when they're ready, let them know what they can expect from you: your love and support, your commitment to caring for their physical needs, and your responsibility to God as a father to teach them about Him and His Word.

Kids may not admit it, but they want direction and boundaries. Let wisdom guide you as you seek the balance between sharing similar experiences and giving them their own space and experience.

*Trust in the LORD with all your heart and do not lean on your
own understanding. In all your ways acknowledge
Him, and He will make your paths straight.*
PROVERBS 3:5–6 NASB

BE WORTH FOLLOWING

If you want to build a ship, don't drum up people to collect wood and don't assign them tasks and work, but rather teach them to long for the endless immensity of the sea.

ANTOINE DE SAINT-EXUPÉRY

You will have a variety of types of interactions with your children—every level of communication from elevator talk to soul-baring intimacy. They look to you when they're not sure what to think about a new person or situation.

As the first authority in your kids' lives, ask yourself this essential question: Am I worth following? You're the boss, but are you a good boss? One measure of that is your level of influence. You're going to impact your kids, but will it be for better or worse?

Jesus is the best possible model. His closest followers believed without a doubt that He was for them, not against them. They trusted that any instructions He gave were for their benefit. Follow His lead: Ask but don't order. Be direct. Be clear. Be there.

Two are better than one, because they have a good return for their labor: If either of them falls down, one can help the other up.

ECCLESIASTES 4:9–10 NIV

EMPATHY FOR ENEMIES

Tolerance isn't about not having beliefs. It's about how your
beliefs lead you to treat people who disagree with you.
TIM KELLER

A surefire recipe for conflict is having persons with differing
views discuss a tough topic. That's the harsh reality of a
broken world. One of the best ways you can prepare your kids
to be salt and light in it is to teach them how to handle people
with whom they don't agree.

First, remind them that people can be confused, mean, and
just plain wrong, but that Jesus still loves them. The real enemy
is Satan, who uses every trick in the book to get people to hate
God and ignore Jesus.

Then give them a biblical understanding of tolerance. Many
folks put it as the highest virtue, above truth and loving God.
Teach your kids that it is respectful to listen courteously to others
who don't believe the same things they do, but that they don't
have to agree with those beliefs.

"To you who are willing to listen, I say, love your enemies!
Do good to those who hate you. Bless those who
curse you. Pray for those who hurt you."
LUKE 6:27–28 NLT

SAY THANK YOU

When it comes to life, the critical thing is whether you take things for granted or take them with gratitude.

G. K. CHESTERTON

One of the first things you should teach your kids is to say "Thank you." Even though it will at first be used as an automatic response when someone gives them something, over time it can become an expression of a way of life.

Gratitude is more than good manners. It counteracts self-pity and promotes contentment. It's at the heart of the Christian life. Over and over the Bible expresses thanks to God and encourages all His people to join in. Whether it's by song or prayer or joyous exclamation, God deserves all the gratitude we can muster.

Make a habit of expressing thanks. Beyond dinner and bedtime prayers, let your kids know when you are thankful. It could be for something as simple as a rainbow or for something bigger, like a new job. Tell them that though you work hard and try your best, it is God who provides and God who deserves to be thanked for all the good things in life.

Devote yourselves to prayer, being watchful and thankful.

COLOSSIANS 4:2 NIV

WHAT YOUR WORDS DON'T SAY

If language was given to men to conceal their thoughts,
then gesture's purpose was to disclose them.
JOHN NAPIER

Although words make up the bulk of our communication, something else has greater impact: body language. Nonverbal communication—the messages we send without words—speaks a lot louder than words.

Before kids even learn to speak, they use gestures, facial expressions, and body positions to tell you how they really feel. This continues throughout our lives, and when words don't match up with actions, people believe actions. Tone and posture matter, so use them wisely to make sure your message gets through.

When we're struggling to speak clearly, body language can send messages of respect and comfort (or their opposites). It shows that we value the other person. Teach your kids the importance of a firm handshake, eye contact, table manners, good hygiene, walking with confidence (even if they aren't confident), and sitting with the kid who is alone at the lunch table.

What are worthless and wicked people like? They are constant
liars, signaling their deceit with a wink of the eye,
a nudge of the foot, or the wiggle of fingers.
PROVERBS 6:12–13 NLT

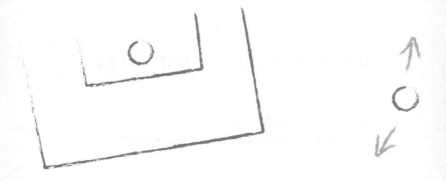

SESSION 4 PLAYBOOK:

Goals of Communication

CATCH 'EM DOING GOOD

Winning doesn't always mean being first. Winning means you're doing better than you've done before.
BONNIE BLAIR

Communication is the lifeblood of any relationship. It keeps things flowing the way blood does in the body. The Bible shows a number of ways you can communicate effectively with your family to promote biblical knowledge and principles, to demonstrate love and affection, and to encourage a high standard of conduct—all of which make God happy and bless your family.

Make a habit of randomly taking a walk around and seeing what your kids are up to. You don't have to be stealthy about it, nor do you have to interrupt what they're doing—although, when they're little, your kids will probably ask, so tell them, "Just trying to catch you guys doing good."

Look for specific things to praise. Just saying "Great job!" won't mean much compared with "I just saw you sharing your snack with your brother. Nice!" Then watch as communication becomes motivation for better behavior.

Let us think of ways to motivate one another
to acts of love and good works.
HEBREWS 10:24 NLT

BUILD 'EM UP

Good words are worth much and cost little.
GEORGE HERBERT

A father's words of praise are like a multivitamin for his child's soul. But they only work if your life matches up with them. Kids smell hypocrisy like it's stuck to the bottom of their shoes, and if they sniff it on you, they'll still love you, but trust will be lost. You shouldn't expect perfection from yourself any more than you expect it from them, but you should set the standard for integrity in words and deeds.

To that end, there are a few phrases you might need to introduce to your vocabulary: "I love you," "I was wrong," and "Please forgive me." Your kids will know whether you mean them, but their value to your communication with them can't be overstated. If your words come in the context of a habit of loving affection, your kids will be drawn toward you, ready to listen.

Let no unwholesome word proceed from your mouth, but only such a word as is good for edification according to the need of the moment, so that it will give grace to those who hear.
EPHESIANS 4:29 NASB

SHOW 'EM GRACE

Half the world is composed of people who have something
to say and can't, and the other half who have
nothing to say and keep on saying it.
ROBERT FROST

God knows we need grace. The prime example is salvation,
where Jesus gave us a gift we don't deserve and could never
earn. But the cross was only the first layer in a pattern of grace
that covers your entire life. God's grace is always available,
always effective—but it's never automatic.

Just as you had to cooperate with God by deciding to accept
His gift, you have to choose to bring grace into your home.
When your home thrives on grace, salvation becomes more than
a moment, instead extending God's love, power, and freedom
into everyday life.

Grace helps you focus on what matters most with your kids—
having a relationship that points them, directly and indirectly,
to God. Grace allows your kids to be different, open about their
feelings and thoughts, and free to make mistakes. Set the tone
of grace that makes that possible.

*Let your speech always be with grace, seasoned with salt,
that you may know how you ought to answer each one.*
COLOSSIANS 4:6 NKJV

PUT 'EM FIRST

When you do the common things in life in an uncommon way,
you will command the attention of the world.
GEORGE WASHINGTON CARVER

Putting your kids first is a basic requirement of parenting, but there's a big difference between making decisions based on their highest good and letting them run your life. There will be times when you have to play the part of Uncool Dad—not Angry Dad or Best Bud Dad, but the guy who holds the line.

In those moments, do your children know that you love them no matter what? That doesn't mean you like everything they do (you won't) or agree with everything they say (you won't). Your kids can frustrate, disappoint, and anger you in all kinds of ways. It's all right to tell them they've done so, but when that conversation is finished, let them know you still love them. They may know that on some fundamental level, but it will be especially important at that point to remind them.

God's love is others-oriented but always goes hand in hand with His truth.

Don't be selfish; don't try to impress others.
Be humble, thinking of others as better than yourselves.
PHILIPPIANS 2:3 NLT

CALL 'EM UP

Success is not final, failure is not fatal:
It is the courage to continue that counts.
WINSTON CHURCHILL

First Corinthians 13, the famous "Love Chapter," sets a daunting standard. Your best shot at it is to let God love through you by helping you find a balance of compassion and truth. With your kids, loving well means continuing to do so when they've done wrong.

There's a difference of intention between calling someone out and calling someone up. In both cases, you let them know they've messed up. Calling someone *out* is to indict a person for having a character problem, as if he is incapable of doing right. But calling someone *up* is to remind him that he is capable of doing better. With calling out, you say, "Get it together or else." With calling up, you say, "You can improve; how can I help?"

Up versus *out* is the key to loving—especially your children—like Jesus loves you.

*Love. . .does not rejoice in iniquity, but rejoices in
the truth; bears all things, believes all things,
hopes all things, endures all things.*
1 CORINTHIANS 13:4, 6–7 NKJV

FREE 'EM UP

Politeness is a sign of dignity, not subservience.
THEODORE ROOSEVELT

L egalism has been a problem for Christians since the early days of the church. Anyone who thinks you need Jesus plus something else (Jesus plus sacrifices, Jesus plus service, Jesus plus rule following) is teaching a false gospel (Colossians 2:6–23). Following rules helps keep an orderly home and society, but in the Christian life, it should not be at the expense of grace. That's the message of the Gospel.

Introduce your children to Paul, whose obsession with the rules made him dangerous. That all changed when he met Jesus and went from religion to relationship. Any rules you present for your family should be couched in terms of relationship.

There's room in a grace-filled home for family preferences regarding media tastes or fashion or jokes. Debate requires biblical principles, but no Jesus juking. Introduce your kids to other people living out their relationship with Jesus so they'll know it's not just your home that handles things in a biblical manner.

It is for freedom that Christ has set us free. Stand firm, then, and do not let yourselves be burdened again by a yoke of slavery.
GALATIANS 5:1 NIV

PUSH 'EM ONWARD

Success consists of getting up just
one more time than you fall.
OLIVER GOLDSMITH

Your first instinct as a dad is to protect your children from all dangers, but you soon learn that it's impossible to do so. Watching your kids fail or seeing them hurting is gut churning, but it's crucial to let them learn how to think about setbacks in a constructive way.

After offering comfort, the best thing you can do is teach your kids resilience. Help them slow down and think about what has happened. Lead them in prayer, asking God to comfort them and shed light on the situation.

Remind them that failure isn't permanent. The only time they should use words like *always* and *never* is with God. He is always in control, always for them, always able to guide them through. He is never unaware, never uncaring, never unloving.

All Scripture is inspired by God and is useful to teach us what is true and to make us realize what is wrong in our lives. It corrects us when we are wrong and teaches us to do what is right. God uses it to prepare and equip his people to do every good work.
2 TIMOTHY 3:16–17 NLT

113

BEAR 'EM UP

Every action in our lives touches on some
chord that will vibrate in eternity.
EDWIN HUBBELL CHAPIN

God doesn't waste our experiences, especially the bad ones. Either He uses your hardship to help you empathize with someone else's similar pain, or He teaches you humility so you can help and not judge others for their mistakes and sins.

You'll recognize some of your children's mistakes because you made the same ones when you were a kid. They'll drive you crazy because you want them to be better than you were, but don't let familiarity breed contempt. Other mistakes will be brand-new, errors you'd never even thought of. In both cases, you have to be deliberate in extending grace.

When Paul spoke of bearing each other's burdens, he was specifically referring to helping one another deal with the consequences of sin "in a spirit of gentleness" (Galatians 6:1 NKJV). This approach will bring healing to your kids and restoration of their walk with God. Furthermore, it will be a strong witness to the world.

Carry each other's burdens, and in this
way you will fulfill the law of Christ.
GALATIANS 6:2 NIV

STRATEGY SESSION 5:

PROPER NUTRITION

DIGGING FOR GOLD

The longer you read the Bible, the more you will like it; it will grow sweeter and sweeter; and the more you get into the spirit of it, the more you will get into the spirit of Christ.

WILLIAM ROMAINE

The Bible is a dad's instructional manual—which can mean that though you ought to be referring to it regularly, you might be more likely to set it aside and try to wing it.

The research to support the Bible's authenticity and reliability is strong and readily available, but Scripture itself testifies to its power: "All Scripture is God-breathed and is useful for teaching, rebuking, correcting and training in righteousness" (2 Timothy 3:16 NIV).

God wants to speak to you through His Word. That alone should excite you, but think of it like this: to be the best father you can be, you need to be the best man you can be, and to do that, you need to learn what the ultimate Father has to say to you.

I remember the days of old; I meditate on all Your works; I muse on the work of Your hands.

PSALM 143:5 NKJV

SOUL BREAD

The Bible, as a revelation from God, was not designed to give us all the information we might desire, nor to solve all the questions about which the human soul is perplexed, but to impart enough to be a safe guide to the haven of eternal rest.

ALBERT BARNES

God's Word has direction for you. It feeds your soul and gives you wisdom, direction, and insight. If you haven't made Bible reading a regular habit, start today: ten minutes in the Gospel of John. Do ten minutes every day till you finish.

If it's hard to understand, that's okay. Ask God to help you, and try different translations or study Bibles or an app. Missing a day is okay; just pick it up the next day. Don't let that missed day convince you that you're wasting your efforts.

Use the time-tested process of observation, interpretation, and application. As you read, ask three questions: *What does it say? What does it mean?* and *What does it mean to me?* It takes work at first, but you'll benefit, and so will your kids—when they see your ready wisdom and good example.

Show me how you work, GOD; school me in your ways.
PSALM 25:4 MSG

CAN YOU AFFORD NOT TO?

Prayer girds human weakness with divine strength,
turns human folly into heavenly wisdom, and gives
to troubled mortals the peace of God.
CHARLES H. SPURGEON

Who has time for prayer? You know you should pray regularly, but in the busyness of life, focusing on God and concentrating on listening to Him can sound like another job, one you can put off without serious repercussions. Or can you?

A busy day (and as a father, there are many) actually requires prayer, just as your car requires gas. Prayer is the most underrated tool in your box because it gives you God's ear. He waits to hear from you, not like some needy friend but as the sovereign Lord of the universe, willing and able to help you.

To let busyness come between you and Him is a mistake on par with ignoring that clunking under the hood until you're stranded by the side of the road in the middle of nowhere. Of course, unlike your engine, God would still be right there with you, waiting to help.

*"We do not present our supplications before You because of
our righteous deeds, but because of Your great mercies."*
DANIEL 9:18 NKJV

BARRIERS TO PRAYER

If you find your life of prayer to be always so short and
so easy and so spiritual as to be without cost and strain
and sweat to you, you may depend upon it,
you have not yet begun to pray.
ALEXANDER WHYTE

There is always something to pray about. That's why Paul said to "pray without ceasing" (1 Thessalonians 5:17 NKJV). Jesus said to pray, so not doing so is disobedience. But what gets in the way of your prayer life? Certain behaviors that come from being too busy build barriers that neutralize prayer's power.

Is confessing sin to God a regular habit? Does prayer feel like a duty? Is there something He has called you to do that you haven't? Unresolved conflict? All of those make it hard to pray.

Prayer reminds you that God is on the throne. That provides perspective on all other issues. Prayer helps you deal with those issues so that you can not only survive the busyness but excel in the midst of it.

This is the confidence which we have before Him, that,
if we ask anything according to His will, He hears us.
1 JOHN 5:14 NASB

HOLY GHOST BUILDING

We cannot give our hearts to God
and keep our bodies for ourselves.
ELISABETH ELLIOT

Regular exercise is an important component of a well-rounded life. You may love working out, or you might be trying to figure out something you can stand doing. If you're married, you've likely been on any number of diets, and maybe you've settled on something that works.

For most guys, the key to exercise is making it sustainable or, if possible, fun. Set realistic goals for yourself and maintain habits that feel normal. Find that balance between being comfortably soft (think huggable!) and reasonably fit. Long live the dad bod!

Make sure that the time you spend exercising doesn't take away from being there for your family. And make sure your focus is on your workout, not on the mirrors or other people.

Bottom line: take care of the Holy Spirit's temple (1 Corinthians 6:19–20). Good health increases your chances of being able to serve God when He sends you. That includes being there for your family.

"Physical training is good, but training for godliness is much better, promising benefits in this life and in the life to come."
1 TIMOTHY 4:8 NLT

WIRED FOR RELATIONSHIP

Jesus said, "Greater things of these you shall do. . ."
Become a peace builder, a bridge builder, not a destroyer,
and the way you do that is through friendships and
relationships, and through authentic character.

RAVI ZACHARIAS

While you can't guarantee your kids' decisions for Christ, you can make sure they know about Him. When they're little, start talking to them about all the things God created and how good He is. As they grow older, look for connections between their interests and biblical perspectives on those topics.

Talk to your kids about all of God's blessings, not just at dinner or before bed, but as you go through the ups and downs of the day. Make sure they know that families were His idea, and talk about how good it is to be in a loving family.

Lead your kids in worship and Bible study. Find age-appropriate ways to teach them what the Bible has to say, and let that be an introduction to the ways of the world around them.

*Most important of all, continue to show deep love for
each other, for love covers a multitude of sins.*
1 PETER 4:8 NLT

WHAT A RELIEF

We may regret what our sins do to our testimony and the evil
effect on others, but we are little concerned because the
fellowship with God is broken. This makes for shallow
and inadequate confession because we have
not touched the heart of the trouble.

VANCE HAVNER

No one is perfect, so we all need grace. We receive grace
when we confess our sins and repent. Make sure your kids
understand the key terms.

Confess just means using words to agree with someone—in
the case of sin, it means to agree with God that you've sinned.

Repent means to turn from something—to turn from sin and
to God. When you turn to God, you will see how to make things
right with people.

Confession is a game changer. You lead your kids in confession, but when you also do it when you've wronged them,
it removes the element of superiority. It also changes you, un-
burdening you of guilt, helping you to walk in the truth of the
Gospel, and leading your kids on the same path.

*If we confess our sins, He is faithful and righteous to forgive us
our sins and to cleanse us from all unrighteousness.*

1 JOHN 1:9 NASB

FAMILY EXPERT

It is a wise father that knows his own child.

WILLIAM SHAKESPEARE

No one should know your family better than you do. God made you the bottom line at home, like a team owner hiring a coach to scout and train players in whom he is heavily invested. The best coaches are the ones who care about their athletes as more than just players but as whole people. Games may be won and lost, but that's secondary to building character.

Learn what you need to know about your kids: their needs, temperaments, experiences, fears, joys, challenges, successes. Read what you have to, talk to wise people, and pay attention to your kids. Ask them revealing questions like, "What would you do with a million bucks?" or "What's your favorite _____ (sport, book, movie, branch of quantum physics)?"

Find out your kid's wiring—introvert or extrovert, pioneer or nurturer—and his love language, and then use that knowledge as you interact with him. It'll take some work, but the returns will be worth it.

For though I am free from all men, I have made myself
a servant to all, that I might win the more.
1 CORINTHIANS 9:19 NKJV

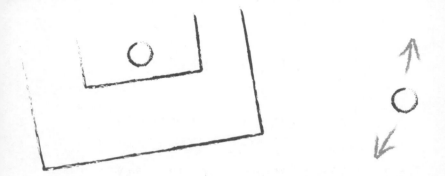

SESSION 5 PLAYBOOK 1:

Spiritual Fruit

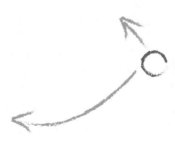

BEING FRUITFUL

God prefers fruit of the Spirit over religious nuts.
ADRIAN ROGERS

Once you receive Christ, the Holy Spirit is your supernatural helper, guiding you to become more like Jesus. The Spirit's work is to produce what the Bible calls the "fruit of the Spirit" in you.

The great thing about the work of the Holy Spirit is that it's *His* work—not yours. Picture a ripe apple hanging from a bough. Did the tree work to make it, sweating and straining, or is its production just part of an apple tree doing what apple trees do?

That's how the Spirit works in you. You can't produce spiritual fruit on your own. Your job is to make room for Him to grow the fruit. You do that by making sure you're living out your faith—putting God first in every part of your life, yielding to His authority, and taking every opportunity to get rid of the "old man" (your pre-Christ habits and attitudes). That's how you develop the fruit the Spirit wants to produce.

> *The fruit of the Spirit is love, joy, peace, longsuffering,*
> *kindness, goodness, faithfulness, gentleness,*
> *self-control. Against such there is no law.*
> GALATIANS 5:22–23 NKJV

LOVE

I want the love that cannot help but love; loving,
like God, for the very sake of love.

A. B. SIMPSON

Asking kids about love leads to a fascinating look inside their thoughts. You'll get surprising insight that touches on the way God loves us—completely sold out for our highest good—and unsurprising body language, with girls blushing and boys squirming like they have lobsters in their shorts. It's adorable (but don't embarrass them by telling them that).

Describe in age-appropriate ways how the world's kind of love is different from the love they'll find in the Bible. The first kind centers on feelings and happiness, both of which come and go and aren't anything on which to base lasting relationships.

God's love, though, is a choice He made (and still makes) to do the best He can for all of His children. His love can be trusted because He will never stop loving them. In response, we do our best to love people the way God does.

We know and rely on the love God has for us. God is love.
Whoever lives in love lives in God, and God in them.
1 JOHN 4:16 NIV

JOY

The man or woman who is wholly or joyously surrendered
to Christ can't make a wrong choice—
any choice will be the right one.
A. W. TOZER

oy means happiness and gladness. While both the world and the Bible mean basically the same thing by "joy," there's a huge difference when it comes to how joy works. The world's version is based on circumstances. You only feel as much joy as your situation allows—and joy flies out the window when hard times come.

For Christians who hold tight to Jesus, though, joy doesn't leave when something bad happens. That's because the joy of Christ is based on spiritual circumstances that won't change. If the worst-case scenario happens and you get eaten by a rhino on the way to work, your kids can still take comfort in knowing they will see you again in heaven.

And for all the hard things that happen in life, godly joy always gives hope because the Holy Spirit will never leave us.

We also pray that you will be strengthened with all his glorious power so you will have all the endurance and patience you need. May you be filled with joy.
COLOSSIANS 1:11 NLT

PEACE

Peace comes when there is no cloud between us and God.
Peace is the consequence of forgiveness, God's removal of
that which obscures His face and so breaks union with Him.

CHARLES H. BRENT

The world can't generate lasting peace of any sort, and that's because it wants nothing to do with Jesus, the One who died to make peace with God. Without Jesus, all people are stuck in factory setting—desperately wishing for peace and unable to find anything that lasts because of sin.

God's prophets conveyed the Lord's disdain for those who say, "Everything's cool," and put Band-Aids on broken legs (or hearts). We can experience momentary peace by resolving momentary conflicts, but only Jesus can resolve the ultimate conflict, the gap between us and God.

Once He does, though, the Spirit brings peace. Clear the way for Him to produce fruit: rejoice in who God is, bring Him all your fears and worries in prayer, fill your mind with His truth, and think about good things (Philippians 4:6–8).

For the mind set on the flesh is death,
but the mind set on the Spirit is life and peace.

ROMANS 8:6 NASB

PATIENCE

The key to everything is patience. You get the chicken
by hatching the egg, not by smashing it.
ARNOLD H. GLASGOW

Patience is in short supply these days. Even among Christians there's a half-serious accusation that when things are going sideways, it's because someone has been praying for patience for us. We know we need it to deal with life in calm, godly ways, but it seems it can only be learned through trials and hardship.

Biblically that makes sense. God is incredibly patient, waiting for people to come to Jesus (2 Peter 3:9), and His people are supposed to be patient in living life for Christ, witnessing, and hoping for loved ones to come to the cross.

Keep that larger picture in mind when patience is called for, especially with your children. Learn the lessons God is trying to teach you about withholding snap judgments and being critical. Instead, focus on hanging in there with your kids; that will show them God's love in a way they just won't find in the world around them.

We do not want you to become lazy, but to imitate those who
through faith and patience inherit what has been promised.
HEBREWS 6:12 NIV

KINDNESS

Kindness has converted more sinners
than zeal, eloquence, or learning.
FREDERICK W. FABER

T he peace and patience the Holy Spirit brings into your life helps pave the way for kindness. When the Bible talks about kindness, it uses words like "show" (2 Samuel 9:1) or "put on" (Colossians 3:12). That suggests that kindness requires action. You can think kind thoughts about someone, but the fruit of the Spirit works both *in* you and *through* you—so that you end up showing kindness to that person.

When it's hard to be kind—and sometimes it is—think about what might be blocking the Spirit's work in you. According to Paul, you need to get rid of "bitterness, rage, anger, harsh words, and slander" and instead "be kind to each other, tenderhearted, forgiving one another, just as God through Christ has forgiven you" (Ephesians 4:31–32 NLT).

For this very reason, giving all diligence, add to your faith virtue,
to virtue knowledge, to knowledge self-control, to self-control
perseverance, to perseverance godliness, to godliness
brotherly kindness, and to brotherly kindness love.
2 PETER 1:5–7 NKJV

GOODNESS

Few things are more infectious than a godly lifestyle.
The people you rub shoulders with every day need
that kind of challenge. Not prudish. Not preachy.
Just cracker jack clean living. Just honest to
goodness, bone-deep, non-hypocritical integrity.
CHUCK SWINDOLL

While goodness is closely related to kindness, being good centers on living out righteousness—what God says is the right thing to do. The summary statement on doing what's right tells us to love our neighbors as ourselves.

Practicing this toward your kids is easy, but getting them to do good things for each other is a different kettle of fish. While you're trying to sort that one out, deal with the idea of reciprocity—giving to get.

From a Christian standpoint, it's dangerous to do good things for others with the thought that they will return the favor. That's not how Jesus operated. He promoted the idea of doing good because it pleases God—and that's enough. Furthermore, if there were anything good you could do to earn God's favor, you wouldn't need the cross.

For this light within you produces only
what is good and right and true.
EPHESIANS 5:9 NLT

FAITHFULNESS

God has been faithful time and again to surround me with
people that sharpen me and that make me better.

TOBYMAC

To be faithful is to be reliable and trustworthy, and no one
meets those requirements more completely than God.

Every person places faith in something. Before you came
to Christ, you put your faith in your desires, the things you
thought mattered most. And then you understood that your
righteousness was like a filthy rag before God's righteousness,
and you knew you'd misplaced your faith.

Some people place faith in faith itself—but faith by itself can't
save anyone. Only Jesus Christ can save us. Only He deserves our
faith, our trust in who He is and what He did for us on the cross.

In return for His continuing faithfulness—His reliability in
every situation we face to stay true to Himself and do what is
right—we offer Him our faith, which the Holy Spirit produces
in us when we trust God.

*God is faithful. He will not allow the temptation to be more
than you can stand. When you are tempted, he will
show you a way out so that you can endure.*

1 CORINTHIANS 10:13 NLT

GENTLENESS

Nothing is so strong as gentleness,
nothing so gentle as real strength.
FRANCIS DE SALES

Gentleness and humility go together like burgers and fries. Some think that gentleness, which the Bible also calls meekness, means being a wimp—that people, particularly your kids, can walk all over you. But they misunderstand. Meekness is strength controlled by grace.

Jesus is the perfect example of gentleness. Think of Him in the temple, rousting the merchants and tipping over their tables. He could have just waved a hand and blasted them all back to the Stone Age, but He controlled His anger for the purpose of defending God's holiness and justice for the worshippers the merchants were fleecing.

When you serve your family, forsaking self-interest and fighting for their highest good, you exhibit gentleness. When you correct them in love, seeking truthful unity and restoration, it's because the Spirit is producing gentleness in you.

Be patient with difficult people. Gently instruct those who oppose the truth. Perhaps God will change those people's hearts, and they will learn the truth.
2 TIMOTHY 2:24–25 NLT

SELF-CONTROL

*If we know that the aim of the Holy Spirit is to lead man to
the place of self-control, we shall not fall into passivity
but shall make good progress in spiritual life.*
WATCHMAN NEE

Even as you take on more of Christ's characteristics—the
fruits of the Spirit you've been reading about—you will still
need the power of the Holy Spirit in you to resist old habits and
tendencies.

Self-control means you mount an ongoing resistance to the
"works of the flesh," an unpleasant list found just before the
roster of the Holy Spirit's work in you (Galatians 5:19–23 NKJV).
The Spirit gives you the strength to say no to those deeds and
the desires that fuel them.

In a spiritual sense, we're all farmers. We either sow seeds
that result in corrupt deeds, or we sow to the Spirit, reaping
the "everlasting life" of the Spirit (Galatians 6:8 NKJV). Sowing
properly is a lifelong battle, but because of Jesus, you are on
the winning side. Sow your Spirit seeds in confidence, in your
own life, and in the hearts of your children.

*For the Spirit God gave us does not make us timid,
but gives us power, love and self-discipline.*
2 TIMOTHY 1:7 NIV

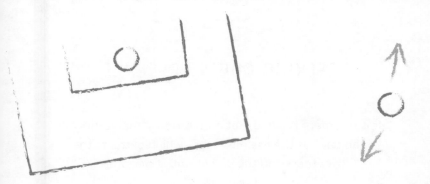

SESSION 5 PLAYBOOK 2:

Studying Truth

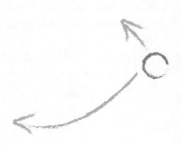

SEEKING GOD'S PRESENCE

*It is not mere reading, but meditation—"meditation all
the day," as the psalmist says—which extracts the
sweetness and the power out of Scripture.*
JAMES STALKER

The Bible repeatedly speaks of seeking God's presence. What does that mean? After all, God is everywhere, so in one sense, He is always present. And God is always with you as a Christian, just as He promised (Matthew 28:20).

Seeking God's presence means getting face-to-face with Him (not literally—not yet!), trusting and looking to Him with intention each day. As Paul wrote, "Set your mind on things above" (Colossians 3:2 NKJV).

We usually seek things we've lost, like keys or the other sock. But God isn't lost. However, if you don't intentionally and consistently look for Him and trust Him as you face life's challenges, you will be lost. So biblical meditation isn't zoning out but is homing in on God, learning to think of Him in the busyness of life. Philippians 4:8 offers several ways for you to do that.

*Fix your thoughts on what is true, and honorable, and right,
and pure, and lovely, and admirable. Think about things
that are excellent and worthy of praise.*
PHILIPPIANS 4:8 NLT

THINK ABOUT TRUTH

Where I found truth, there I found my God,
who is the truth itself.
AUGUSTINE

Making sense of life, figuring out its meaning and purpose, is all about the search for truth. Naturally, it matters where you look. Go back two thousand years to the Praetorium in Jerusalem. There Jesus said, "Everyone who is of the truth hears My voice," to which Pilate responded, "What is truth?" (John 18:37–38 NKJV). God is truth, so when the world rejects Him, it can never know truth.

You, however, have access to the most remarkable record of God's truth. The Bible is God's message to all of us, reliable and consistent in thought, content, and purpose. The Old Testament says thousands of times, "And God said." That alone makes it different.

But the story it tells is mind-blowing: God created a good world, man ruined it, and God set out a plan to win us back from sin and death. You want the truth? You can handle it—it's in God's Word.

He brought us to life using the true Word,
showing us off as the crown of all his creatures.
JAMES 1:18 MSG

137

REFLECT ON RIGHTEOUSNESS

Forgiveness is negative. Righteousness is positive.
Forgiveness is you may go. Righteousness is you may come.
TIM KELLER

When Paul said to meditate on what is honorable and right, he was speaking of the nobility of following God. As a believer, you need to take life seriously because God does. What you do matters to God and to others.

Living in light of eternity—aware that life is short, that heaven and hell are real, and that God will hold you accountable for what you've done with what He has given you—is crucial. What you can't afford to do, however, is take yourself too seriously.

Think of how Jesus interacted with people. He never came at them from a position of His own moral superiority (though He alone could have) but always spoke to them where they were at in life. Furthermore, He never compromised the message. He forgave but then pointed the forgiven toward righteousness. That's the tone to shoot for, especially with your kids.

The path of the righteous is level; you, the Upright One, make the way of the righteous smooth.
ISAIAH 26:7 NIV

PONDER WHAT IS PURE

*He who loves with purity considers not the gift
of the lover, but the love of the giver.*
THOMAS À KEMPIS

Purity suggests innocence, something uncontaminated and clean, free of hidden agendas and ulterior motives. You probably thought of purity when you looked at your kids as infants. The protector in you has suffered as their innocence has broken down over the years. Whether it's because of their own willful behavior or the cruelty of others, it's heartbreaking to see them realize that the world is broken and harmful.

However, because of Jesus, you can strive for His purity, making a commitment to pleasing God that cleanses you of sin and protects you from spiritual pollution. Though it's a constant battle—against worry and sexual immorality and fear and anger—it's one you can win by arming yourself with prayer, God's Word, Christian fellowship, and faith that, with Christ, you are an overcomer.

*That means killing off everything connected with that way of
death: sexual promiscuity, impurity, lust, doing whatever you
feel like whenever you feel like it, and grabbing whatever
attracts your fancy. That's a life shaped by things
and feelings instead of by God.*
COLOSSIANS 3:5 MSG

APPRECIATE THE ADMIRABLE

Since love grows within you, so beauty grows.
For love is the beauty of the soul.
AUGUSTINE

True beauty appeals to heart and soul, not just the eye. The world is consumed with "the lust of the flesh, the lust of the eyes, and the pride of life" (1 John 2:16 NKJV)—physical pleasures, material goods, and pride in possessions and accomplishments. The messages sent through marketing campaigns and social media paint an obsession with appearances—false ideals and dangerously unrealistic expectations for our kids to emulate.

Guide your children toward true beauty. The Bible makes it clear that physical beauty fades with time, whether in a person or in a flower, and that true beauty is something inside that God finds precious—a gentle, calm spirit. With His help, that's a goal anyone can pursue and achieve.

Even in this sin-broken world, you can still find beauty—you just have to keep your eyes peeled. Feed your soul with God's Word, and guide your kids toward His standards of what is worthwhile.

"The LORD does not see as man sees; for man looks at the outward appearance, but the LORD looks at the heart."
1 SAMUEL 16:7 NKJV

EXAMINE THE EXCELLENT

> How wonderful to know that when Jesus Christ speaks to you
> and to me, he enables you to understand yourself, to die to
> that self because of the cross, and brings the real you to birth.
>
> RAVI ZACHARIAS

Your kids are growing up in a world with a skewed view of virtue and excellence. There are those who find ultimate value in accomplishments like material accumulation or moving among society's highest, but more recent cultural movements make tolerance the highest virtue—that there is no such thing as objective truth, that we each must make our own.

Your kids will take mental notes on what you say is worthy of praise—things such as modesty, moral excellence, purity, celebrating friends and family, and being different from the world.

Steep your thoughts in God's Word, and let those thoughts drive your interactions with your children. When you memorize scripture and study the Bible, you're preparing yourself to prepare your kids to follow God and stand up to a world that opposes Him.

He has given us great and precious promises. These are the
promises that enable you to share his divine nature and
escape the world's corruption caused by human desires.
2 PETER 1:4 NLT

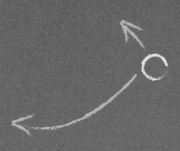

STRATEGY SESSION 6:

DISCIPLINARY TRAINING

BY HOOK OR BY CROOK

> A true shepherd leads the way.
> He does not merely point the way.
> LEONARD RAVENHILL

A shepherd's staff has two practical purposes: first, it extends your reach so you can direct sheep where you want them to go; second, the crook at the end helps you round up sheep that need to be tended to or protected from danger. Before you get a staff for your children, stay on the metaphorical level a bit longer.

David spoke of being comforted by God's rod and staff (often the same tool); that is, he appreciated God keeping him safe and on the right path (Psalm 23:4). That's what Jesus told Peter to do when He restored him—to feed, tend, and protect His sheep (John 21:15–19).

Jesus asks you as a dad to do the same thing with your kids. Being a good shepherd means showing genuine love and affection, providing at times and protecting at others—even protecting your little sheep from themselves at times.

> *The LORD is my shepherd; I have all that I need.*
> PSALM 23:1 NLT

WINNING THE WAR WITHIN

Children are unpredictable. You never know what
inconsistency they are going to catch you in next.
HENRY WARD BEECHER

Self-control sums up the ongoing battle between the Spirit
and the flesh. Jesus will redeem your body at the rapture,
but until that happens (which may be for the rest of your life),
you'll face temptations to do the opposite of what the Holy
Spirit wants you to do. To overcome, you must "walk in the
Spirit" (Galatians 5:16 NKJV).

There are times when that fight gets hard, and you may think,
I didn't sign up for a war; I want peace. God's peace, however,
isn't the absence of conflict but the power to overcome it—"if
you are led by the Spirit" (v. 18). His power leads you like the
engine on a train.

Your kids need you to practice self-control for their security
and support, but also so they can see what it looks like to let
God be God in their own lives.

All things are lawful for me, but all things are not helpful.
All things are lawful for me, but I will not be
brought under the power of any.
1 CORINTHIANS 6:12 NKJV

LEADERS SERVE

If we give God service, it must be because He gives us
grace. We work for Him because He works in us.
CHARLES H. SPURGEON

It's been said that you can tell a lot about a man based on
how he treats kids, waiters, and dogs. He stands to gain no
advantage professionally or socially from any of them, so any
kindness or respect he shows must be the result of his genuine
care for others.

It makes sense, then, that God's great mission for us is to
spread the good news that He volunteered Himself to redeem
anyone who would receive His Son. You give your time and talents because you are grateful for all that God has done for you.

There are side benefits to volunteering. Helping others draws
you closer to God since you're behaving in someone else's best
interest with no thought of being repaid. There is great joy in
knowing you've made a difference with your time and resources.
Your kids will see that you value helping others with no thought
of what you can get in return.

*The generous soul will be made rich, and he who
waters will also be watered himself.*
PROVERBS 11:25 NKJV

THE DANGER OF COULDA, SHOULDA, WOULDA

What to do with a mistake: recognize it,
admit it, learn from it, forget it.
DEAN SMITH

Everyone has regrets. If you think you have lots of regrets as a dad, try to recall what it was like when you were a kid. Regrets pile up like missiles during the Cold War.

Fortunately, faith in Christ enables us to avoid being poisoned by radioactive memories. Your kids will also have regrets. Your job is to keep them from adding "Dad thinks I'm a screwup" to their lists. Yes, they'll screw up, but you can make a huge difference by looking at their effort over their flaws.

Some people think God looks at us with a critical eye, waiting for our next mistake so He can say, "Uh-huh. I knew it." But that's not God's line; it's Satan's. Better to imitate God and show understanding than to be like the devil and set your kids (and yourself) up for failure.

The Lord is not slow about His promise, as some count slowness,
but is patient toward you, not wishing for any to
perish but for all to come to repentance.
2 PETER 3:9 NASB

FREELY SURRENDER

Let God have your life. He can do more with it than you can.
DWIGHT L. MOODY

The Christian life involves an ongoing process of surrender. That's counterintuitive, especially for guys, for whom surrender is right down there with backseat driving and insults to our mothers. But whereas the latter two are deeply offensive, surrender is necessary—and much harder.

Jesus talked about each of us taking up our cross and following Him. The burden He referred to was you—you have to take your selfish attitudes and behaviors, your lust, sin, and anger, and nail them to the cross of Christ. The "old you" must die; that's what you're surrendering.

You surrender to Christ's lordship when you initially come to faith in Him. When you see your sin for what it is, shame and guilt set in, but instead of letting them take hold, you surrender your sin to Christ, and He frees you from shame and guilt. Nevertheless, giving up your rights and letting God rule is an ongoing process. Failure to live in surrender to Christ creates struggle and tension, both within you and with others. If you want your kids to see the importance of surrendering to God, let them see you model it.

Now, just as you accepted Christ Jesus as your Lord,
you must continue to follow him.
COLOSSIANS 2:6 NLT

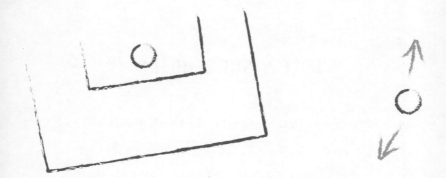

SESSION 6 PLAYBOOK 1:

Priority Checks

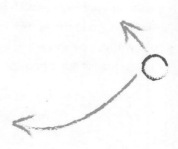

WITH ALL YOUR HEART

For we love not God first, to compel him to love again;
but he loved us first, and gave his Son for us,
that we might see love and love again.

William Tyndale

Loving God with all your heart, soul, and strength sounds impossible. You love the Lord, you love His Word, you love His people, and you love others—but not at all times and seldom with all that you are.

Only Jesus loved God with all that He was at all times. That's an impossible standard to live up to—in your own strength. But in Christ's strength and by His Spirit, you can become more like Him. Jesus made the impossible possible by making you a new creation *in Him* (2 Corinthians 5:17–21). You put your trust in Him to save you, and you must walk "just as He walked" (1 John 2:6 NKJV).

In putting God first, Jesus didn't say you should neglect your family in favor of serving Him (Matthew 10:37). Rather, serving and loving your family is an important way to serve and love Him.

Whoever claims to live in him must live as Jesus did.
1 John 2:6 NIV

YOUR FIRST MINISTRY

There is something ultimate in a father's love, something that
cannot fail, something to be believed against the whole
world. We almost attribute omnipotence to
our father in the days of our childhood.

FREDERICK WILLIAM FABER

If God hasn't called you to the celibate, single life (as He did Paul, for example), then He has called you to be a family man. His instructions are to be fruitful and multiply (Genesis 1:28), not only to make more people but to raise godly people, beginning at home.

Service to God starts with your wife and children. They are your first ministry, established back in Genesis, well before the church came into being. If you are married, your wife takes priority over your kids (Genesis 2:24), then your kids come next. This perspective models for your children God's design for marriage and family. So many of God's purposes and designs are reflected in and modeled through the family that it takes second place in priority after loving Him.

God blessed them: "Prosper! Reproduce! Fill Earth!
Take charge! Be responsible for fish in the sea and birds in the air,
for every living thing that moves on the face of Earth."
GENESIS 1:28 MSG

THE HOUSEHOLD OF GOD

The church is the gathering of God's children, where they can be helped and fed like babies and then guided by her motherly care, grow up to manhood in maturity of faith.
JOHN CALVIN

You have a role to play in God's church. It may not be as a pastor or deacon or teacher, but God wants you to serve in some capacity. It's fine to start out with attendance, listening and learning about what it means to follow Jesus. But that's just the start. Things like giving and serving must follow as you grow in your faith.

Ask God to show you where He wants to plug you in, then get plugged in: "Therefore, whenever we have the opportunity, we should do good to everyone—especially to those in the family of faith" (Galatians 6:10 NLT).

Church should also be a given in your family's schedule. And on the mornings when everyone is dragging, remind them that God deserves your worship among His people. Besides, who knows how God could use what's taught on Sunday during the rest of the week?

Now you are the body of Christ,
and each one of you is a part of it.
1 CORINTHIANS 12:27 NIV

ONE NATION

*It is impossible to rightly govern a nation
without God and the Bible.*
GEORGE WASHINGTON

S ome people, even some Christians, believe there is never a
time for war. But the Bible indicates that there is—and that
peace is often a by-product of battles won. While God's way is
not violent, in a broken world, violence must be employed on
occasion in service of peace.

Some men are called to serve their country as soldiers or
law enforcement officers. All young men should understand
the necessity of being willing to serve their country, not as top
priority, but coming only after God, family, and church.

God established governments and armies to maintain peace
in a disorderly world. In times of peace, that may mean our
duty is only to vote, which we should do—and should explain
the importance of to our kids. Others may be called to lead
in their communities, cities, states, or even countries. And when
a pressing need arises—a natural disaster or neighborhood
crisis—we should be among the first to pitch in and help.

*A time to love and a time to hate;
a time for war and a time for peace.*
ECCLESIASTES 3:8 NASB

WHAT DO YOU DO?

All work, according to God's design, is service.
TIM KELLER

The first thing God did after creating man was give him a job. God designed us to work, to think and then do, in order to create, maintain, and get the most out of the world He made. God made you "a little lower than the angels" and "crowned [you] with glory and honor" (Psalm 8:5 NKJV). That means that whatever you do, you should do it with dignity and honor.

One of the first things we do when we meet another man is ask him what he does. Work is an identifier, not because certain jobs make us better than others, but because God made us to work.

The part of you that as a child made every stick a weapon or tool reflects that drive God put in you for adventure and dominion. You are meant to explore, to challenge yourself, to care for what God has given you, and to be a leader worth following, in the home and on the job.

GOD took the Man and set him down in the Garden of Eden to work the ground and keep it in order.
GENESIS 2:15 MSG

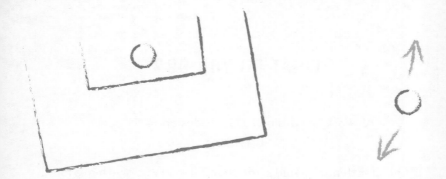

SESSION 6 PLAYBOOK 2:

Money

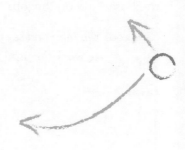

USE MONEY

The world asks, "What does a man own?"
Christ asks, "How does he use it?"
ANDREW MURRAY

Who owns your stuff? According to the Bible, God does. He owns everything (Psalm 24:1). Accepting that fact leads to embracing the most important financial principle in scripture: stewardship. What you own isn't about property rights in God's eyes; it's about taking care of and using what He has given you—beginning with your ability to work.

God owns it all, and He takes care of His people, but we should use what He gives us to build His kingdom; everything else is short term. Earn your money, then use it for God's glory; otherwise, it will use you.

Don't assume anyone else is teaching your kids about money. Establish the principles the Bible gives, but also teach practical tips about money—savings, interest, how credit cards work, and what a budget is. Above all, teach them that their worth isn't in their bank accounts or stock portfolios but in their value to God, who paid the highest price of all to love them.

The earth is the LORD'S, and all it contains,
the world, and those who dwell in it.
PSALM 24:1 NASB

GIVERS AND TAKERS

My father said there were two kinds of people in the world:
givers and takers. The takers may eat better,
but the givers sleep better.
MARLO THOMAS

Earning money is important. What you do with it is even more so. Biblically speaking, there's a good chance you won't make more until you are satisfied making do with less. If your kids see money and not God as the great problem solver, you have a problem, so help them understand what money is for.

Teach your kids that saving honors God, the giver of all good gifts. Get them a piggy bank and encourage them to use it. When they are about age eight, teach them an envelope system, using different envelopes labeled Savings, Tithe, Spend, Gifts, and Clothes.

Coach them in trading off (an ice cream today means less saved for that video game) and smart shopping (the fine print on and messages behind ads). Make money talk part of your everyday conversations, teaching them as you go through real-life situations. Wisdom in money matters is a good witness for God.

The wise have wealth and luxury,
but fools spend whatever they get.
PROVERBS 21:20 NLT

YOU CAN'T OUTGIVE GOD

The more you give, the more comes back to you, because God is the greatest giver in the universe, and He won't let you outgive Him. Go ahead and try. See what happens.

RANDY ALCORN

The wonder of God's economic model is that it enriches the giver, not the hoarder. And it's never about money but about trust that God will take care of you. As Paul noted, "Not that I seek the gift, but I seek the fruit that abounds to your account" (Philippians 4:17 NKJV).

How you handle money is part of your witness for Christ. Bring your kids into your giving and show them how cheerful giving works. Tithing is setting aside the first part of your money for God's church; then you set aside another portion for giving to other causes He lays on your heart.

This goes hand in hand with the biblical commands that we should work for our money and earn it honestly: "Lazy hands make for poverty, but diligent hands bring wealth" (Proverbs 10:4 NIV). Giving shows appreciation for God and His blessings, and trust that He will provide.

Remember this: Whoever sows sparingly will also reap sparingly, and whoever sows generously will also reap generously.

2 CORINTHIANS 9:6 NIV

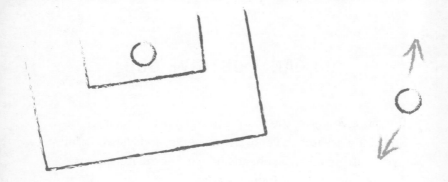

SESSION 6 PLAYBOOK 3:

Disciplines of Discipline

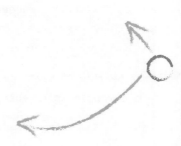

IMITATION AS INTRODUCTION

*Human fatherhood should be molded and modeled on
the pattern of the fatherhood of God.*
WILLIAM BARCLAY

Being a good dad means being like God as you raise your kids. How you see God impacts how your kids will see Him. Know for a fact that just as Jesus has made it possible for you to be more like Him, He has also provided all you need so you can follow your heavenly Father's lead in love, godliness, and discipline.

Being a dad means disciplining your children, but the root of the word *discipline* is "disciple." You are your kids' teacher, guide, and instructor in what it means to follow God. Before you start wondering about things like spanking or grounding, concern yourself with introducing your children to their Maker.

Bring worship into your home, joyfully praising God for His love and good care. Thank Him for all the wonderful ways He has made each of the people in your family. With consistency and the right attitude, you'll demonstrate that discipline is evidence of love.

*Moreover, we have all had human fathers who disciplined us and
we respected them for it. How much more should we
submit to the Father of spirits and live!*
HEBREWS 12:9 NIV

OBJECTIVE: RESPECT

A child who is allowed to be disrespectful to his parents
will not have true respect for anyone.

BILLY GRAHAM

Godly discipline is distinguished by its purpose—never to punish but to promote godly behavior. Chances are, your kids have done things that made you very angry, and if you're honest, you've felt like paying them back for bad behavior.

But God liberates you from taking on something that He will do Himself (Romans 12:19)—and even then, only with those whose decision it is to reject Him. Your job is to instill respect in your kids. Their job is to obey you, but when they don't, you need to understand how to govern your response.

When you discipline your kids, ask yourself, *Is my action helping them choose more wisely in the future?* Will your correction result in protection for your children and those around them? Respond with consequences first, then talk about it later, encouraging them to see how they can do better next time.

Children, do what your parents tell you. This is only right.
"Honor your father and mother" is the first commandment
that has a promise attached to it, namely, "so you
will live well and have a long life."
EPHESIANS 6:1–3 MSG

SET THE STANDARD

It is not what you do for your children, but what
you have taught them to do for themselves,
that will make them successful human beings.

Ann Landers

Paul specifically told fathers not to "provoke [their] children to anger" (Ephesians 6:4 NASB). Why dads? Because God has given you the task of discipling your kids in His ways and holding them accountable when they don't follow them.

What does "provoke" mean? Well, your kids may provoke you by pressing your buttons, but you may not realize that you're doing the same to them. Unless you are consistently praying and checking God's Word for guidance, you can get off course.

Some common ways dads provoke their kids include over-protection, favoritism, discouragement, and one of the all-time list toppers: pressured achievement under the motto "You can always do better." Be careful that your vision for your kids centers on God's best for them, not your fantasies about them being star athletes or concert violinists. God loves you whether or not you achieve worldly success, whether or not you are obedient. Make sure your kids get the same message.

*Fathers, don't exasperate your children by coming down
hard on them. Take them by the hand and lead
them in the way of the Master.*
Ephesians 6:4 MSG

THE ART OF DISTRACTION

In reading the lives of great men, I found that the
first victory they won was over themselves. . .
self-discipline with all of them came first.
HARRY S. TRUMAN

A famous experiment involving marshmallows showed that kids
who resisted the temptation to take more than an allotted
single treat went on to lead happier, healthier lives.

Self-discipline actually hinges on the ability to turn your
attention away from yourself. That's a crucial component of
living a God-pleasing life, so get started training your kids on the
concept. Use the art of distraction—covering the marshmallow,
for example, or putting the phone in a drawer while they do
chores or homework.

We often wait on God for answers to prayer or direction
with a decision. It can be tempting to circumvent an answer
by forging ahead with what we want to do. But then we miss
out on the joy of waiting for God's perfect timing. Start small
with your kids and move forward in the confidence that God is
worth waiting for.

*All athletes are disciplined in their training. They do it to win
a prize that will fade away, but we do it for an eternal prize.*
1 CORINTHIANS 9:25 NLT

INVEST NOW OR PAY LATER

If we never have headaches through rebuking our children,
we shall have plenty of heartaches when they grow up.
CHARLES H. SPURGEON

We tend to shy away from correcting our kids because we're not sure we should be doing it. Sometimes things take care of themselves, and we don't want to be impatient or just plain wrong. Sometimes we can afford to wait on the Lord, but other times we need to respond to a situation. Our attitude is all important as we do either one.

First, make sure you are practicing the discipline you want from your child. Are you doing what God told you to do—seeking His presence, meditating on His Word, praying with expectation, and loving others as yourself? If you are, then dealing with a disobedient child will be easier.

You'll already know that whatever consequences you decide are needed should come from your love and concern for your child's welfare, not from frustration or anger. You know that when you're really hot, you need to cool down before administering discipline.

The purpose of my instruction is that all believers would
be filled with love that comes from a pure heart,
a clear conscience, and genuine faith.
1 TIMOTHY 1:5 NLT

HOLDING THE LINE

We must all suffer one of two things: the pain of discipline
or the pain of regret or disappointment.

JIM ROHN

It's a fact that your kids will need correction. One of your big decisions will be whether to spank them. But it's not a decision you want to make in the heat of the moment. Simply put, you don't want to hurt your kids just because they hurt you.

That goes against Jesus' instruction to turn the other cheek and against your mandate to demonstrate godly responses in tough situations. The Bible makes it clear that if you don't discipline your child, you are failing to love her properly.

The rod is a shepherd's tool for guiding his sheep away from danger. In the context of spanking, it means using an appropriate tool to administer a few hard swats. Your hand should be reserved for holding your child and comforting her after the spanking. God is all about restoration of relationship, and you should be too. If you don't spank, then the rod becomes whatever method works to bring about the same end.

A refusal to correct is a refusal to love;
love your children by disciplining them.
PROVERBS 13:24 MSG

CAUSE AND EFFECT

Love precedes discipline.
JOHN OWEN

Effective discipline requires that you understand what kind of parent you are. Researchers have found four kinds of parents and described the motive for each type: permissive parents are driven by fear, authoritarian ones are characterized by fighting, neglectful parents forsake their kids, and authoritative ones are motivated by fellowship.

Which kind of parent are you? If you aren't sure, consider your motive in discipline. Do you try to avoid conflict with your child (permissive)? Do you dare your kid to go against you (authoritarian)? Are you sure your kids are just being kids and there's nothing to talk about (neglectful)? Or do you seek to guide them toward loving God and His truth more than they love having things their way?

If you model the hardship of discipline as a way of showing love, of guiding your kids toward unwavering trust in God's goodness and faithfulness, you will be fulfilling your calling as a dad.

My son, do not despise the LORD's discipline, and do not resent his rebuke, because the LORD disciplines those he loves, as a father the son he delights in.
PROVERBS 3:11–12 NIV

SHORT-TERM PAIN
AND LONG-TERM GAIN

It is easier to build strong children
than to repair broken men.
FREDERICK DOUGLASS

Take the long view when disciplining your kids. Settle your thoughts about it before you're in the midst of it, because when it's happening, you won't have the bandwidth to come up with a philosophy, and as a result, you'll be reacting, not responding according to a plan.

Scripture makes it clear that those who don't experience God's discipline aren't His legitimate children (Hebrews 12:7–8). The goal of godly discipline is to promote future correct acts rather than punishing past mistakes.

So when being a dad gets hard, stick to your guns. Picture giving your kid the keys and riding along as he starts to head for a cliff. Would you discuss his decision while you're hurtling along at sixty miles per hour? No, you'd yank the wheel or slam the brakes, and then deal with him being mad at you—and be thankful he's still there to get angry.

*No discipline seems pleasant at the time, but painful.
Later on, however, it produces a harvest of righteousness
and peace for those who have been trained by it.*
HEBREWS 12:11 NIV

NATURAL CONSEQUENCES

Nobody ever did, or ever will, escape the
consequences of his choices.
ALFRED A. MONTAPERT

It's a biblical fact that you will reap the consequences of your actions, whether good or bad. Understanding that, however, doesn't mean it's always easy to decide how to respond when your child does something wrong.

Pick your battles. When it's safe, let your kid deal with the consequences of what you know will be a bad choice. Don't talk about anger when your kid is angry; discuss behavior and consequences in a calmer moment.

Highlight the cause and effect of your kid's choices. If she keeps shooting hoops, she's going to get better. If he studies well for the math test, he'll feel more confident. Let your children know their choices affect others too. If he doesn't come home at the arranged time or call, you get worried. Her grandma loves it when she calls just to say hi. Big or small, positive or negative, your kids can learn from their experiences.

The one who sows to his own flesh will from the flesh reap
corruption, but the one who sows to the Spirit
will from the Spirit reap eternal life.
GALATIANS 6:8 NASB

STRATEGY SESSION 7:

GAME TIME

ALL TIME IS QUALITY TIME

The best gift a father can give to his son is the gift of
himself—his time. For material things mean little,
if there is not someone to share them with.
NEIL C. STRAIT

C harles Adams, son of John Quincy Adams, spent a day fishing with his son Brooks. Each of them kept a journal, but the day's events impacted each one differently. Brooks wrote, "Went fishing with my father today, the most glorious day of my life." The entry in his father's journal, however, said, "Went fishing with my son, a day wasted."

All time with you matters to your kids, so it all has quality. If you're invested in each of those moments—shooting hoops, doing homework, building with Legos—they'll remember it. They'll know they matter if you set aside time for them. There's no secret activity or place that's key here, just your engagement.

Special events are fun, but small moments are cherished too. If your kid is talking to you, get face-to-face and listen. When you're leaving work, get ready to fully focus on your family. Every moment matters.

*"There is no greater love than to lay down
one's life for one's friends."*
JOHN 15:13 NLT

STUDIES SAY

There's life, and there's making a living. Family is life.
DENZEL WASHINGTON

One of the joys of the Christian life is when the world seems to catch up with what the Bible says. An example of this comes in the form of research about the effects of dads who are present and engaged in raising their kids.

Without getting wonky about the details, suffice it to say that adults whose dads spent quality time with them when they were kids enjoy better health (including fewer instances of premature aging or cancer), higher IQs, happier work lives, a sense of worth, greater emotional security, and fewer disciplinary issues at school and work.

Babies in the womb can hear a male voice more clearly due to its lower tone. Furthermore, because dads tend to engage less in baby talk, they play a key role in their child's language development. When God told dads to take charge of their children's spiritual development, He clearly arranged human biology to make this possible—if we as dads will just do our part.

The father of godly children has cause for joy.
What a pleasure to have children who are wise.
PROVERBS 23:24 NLT

BE AVAILABLE, BE PRESENT

If you want your children to turn out well, spend twice as much time with them and half as much money.

ABIGAIL VAN BUREN

Being a dad means the days are long but the years fly by. Fortunately, the days seem to have passed when, if most dads weren't at work, they were on the golf course. That's a good development, but even if you want to be there for your kids, you still need to make the time count.

That doesn't necessarily mean planning anything special. It just means preparing yourself on the way home from work to engage with your kids. If you need to take a few extra minutes, even parked in the driveway, to get your workday set aside for the moment, take the time. When you get home, be ready to come in smiling and ready to rumble, and to help your wife with whatever she's got going on.

When you're at work, do your kids have permission to call you whenever they need to? Down the road, would you rather say, "I wish I had" or "I'm glad I did"?

A good man leaves an inheritance to his children's children.

PROVERBS 13:22 NKJV

SHELTERING LOVE

The most important thing a father can do for
his children is to love their mother.

HENRY WARD BEECHER

Both sons and daughters look to their dads for an example of how a good man should behave, especially toward women. Treating your wife with respect, preferring her above everyone else, and displaying affection appropriately gives your son an idea of how to treat a girl and your daughter an idea of how she should be treated. Loving your wife is God's best for all of you.

A note for single dads: you're doing your best to raise godly kids on your own, whether it's due to divorce or being widowed. If you're divorced, though, you can still send an important message to your kids by showing your ex respect, especially if you think she doesn't deserve it. What better example of Christ's love could you possibly give in that frustrating context?

Husbands, likewise, dwell with them with understanding,
giving honor to the wife, as to the weaker vessel,
and as being heirs together of the grace of life,
that your prayers may not be hindered.

1 PETER 3:7 NKJV

PLAY IS THE WORK OF CHILDREN, SO GET TO WORK

You can discover more about a person in an hour of play than in a year of conversation.

PLATO

You've heard the saying "Play is the work of children." When you were a kid, you took what you were doing seriously, whether it was baseball, board games, or just riding bikes around the neighborhood. You wouldn't have thought of it like this, but you were trying on adult roles, taking responsibility, and doing grown-up jobs.

When you play with your kids, fully engage with the world they've created. It might seem totally nonsensical, in which case you can let them be the experts and tell you the rules for a change. Or they might be more serious, based on the stories you've told them about work. Either way, just roll with it.

And roll around *with* them too. Kids love to wrestle with their dads (even if moms squirm when you get near the coffee table or a vase of flowers). Play can teach you a lot about what matters to them.

I recommend having fun, because there is nothing better for people in this world than to eat, drink, and enjoy life.

ECCLESIASTES 8:15 NLT

SPLISH SPLASH

May your coffee be stronger than your toddler!
UNKNOWN

Having a toddler is hard work, but the little ones are also a lot of fun, so all the dirty diapers and messy meals and packing up of a couple hundred pounds of gear just to go to the park can be the counterbalance.

Depending on your work schedule, your best time to engage with your toddler might be first thing in the morning and when you get home in the evening—but take every opportunity. You get used to sleeping a few hours a night surprisingly quickly.

Aside from mealtime, other kid-related tasks like getting dressed, bath time, and bedtime offer great chances to have fun. Make up silly songs about doing chores. Lie down with them and talk when you tuck them in at night (they also love the excuse to stay up past bedtime). God has given you a precious gift in your children, and you honor Him and them by making the most of your time to build relationship with them.

Oh come, let us sing to the LORD!
Let us shout joyfully to the Rock of our salvation.
PSALM 95:1 NKJV

CAN'T WE ALL JUST GET ALONG?

*My father always used to say that when you die, if you've
got five real friends, then you've had a great life.*

LEE IACOCCA

Having friends is a huge part of a kid's life. Some will make
friends easily, others not so much, but it's a good idea to
show them what it means to be a good friend. If you model self-
respect for them, it will go a long way toward helping them feel
comfortable in their own skin. Make it clear that the relationship
game kids start playing in fourth or fifth grade is just plain silly.

Make sure your kids understand that God made them the
way they are for very good reasons, and He doesn't make mistakes. It's okay to go solo when everyone else is pairing up like
twitterpated birds. All people matter to God, and all people have
value, no matter what they look like or where they're from. Let
your children be who God made them to be, and let them know
that the right friends will come along at the right time.

*Don't be concerned for your own good
but for the good of others.*
1 CORINTHIANS 10:24 NLT

LIMITS WILL BE TESTED

By the time a man realizes that maybe his father was right,
he usually has a son who thinks he's wrong.

CHARLES WADSWORTH

Familiarize yourself with the ways your kids use and experience technology and its relentless flow of information and stimulation. You can learn about social media, for example, without succumbing to it yourself, and you should make access to your kids' accounts a condition for their having them. Know their passwords and what's in their folders. Set up filters and time limits on your devices.

Monitoring of devices can set you apart as Cool Dad or Helicopter Dad. You want your kids to experience technology, but you don't want them to endure all the awful things bad people do with it, like identity theft, sex trafficking, and bullying.

You may think, *I trust my kids. I don't need to monitor their viewing.* But have you forgotten what you were like at their age? All kids from about age eight on up operate by the philosophy "What my parents don't know won't hurt me." Your beautiful, trustworthy babies are no different, so take precautions.

Don't waste your time on useless work, mere busywork,
the barren pursuits of darkness.

EPHESIANS 5:11 MSG

BREAKING BREAD
AND BUILDING BONDS

The oldest form of theater is the dinner table. It's got
five or six people, new show every night, same players.
Good ensemble; the people have worked together a lot.

MICHAEL J. FOX

The Bible often mentions the value of breaking bread together, especially in the context of the early church, when fellowship and hearing God's Word were mortar and bricks holding together what God was building. The same goes for your family.

When your kids are little, eating dinner together creates security and belonging, and even teenagers look forward to catching up at the table. Research also shows that you'll all eat healthier too—more fruits and vegetables and fewer sodas and fried foods.

Let your children get to know you too. Ask about them, but also tell them about your day. As a wise person once said, "At dinnertime, grill the food, not your kids." Endless queries are exhausting, just as they would be for you.

That sense of togetherness builds happier, stress-relieving relationships, especially when the things of God are part of regular conversation.

Whether, then, you eat or drink or whatever you do,
do all to the glory of God.
1 CORINTHIANS 10:31 NASB

TEE BALL AND TEA PARTIES

Becoming a father increases your capacity for love and your
level of patience. It opens up another door in a person—
a door which you may not even have known was there.
KYLE MACLACHLAN

When it comes to attending your kids' activities, it's often
a matter of time or energy levels. You want to go to their
game or see their performance at school, but what a week you've
had! Those chances to support them are rarer than you think,
and more fleeting.

You can (and should) make time for yourself to rest and recharge, but being there is part of an implicit promise you made
when you had kids. Family is your first ministry.

Get involved at home. Play your kids' games and watch their
shows with them. It shows investment in what matters to them
and gives you info about what their little eyes are seeing. You
send the message that what they do matters to you.

*Young people, it's wonderful to be young! Enjoy every minute of
it. Do everything you want to do; take it all in. But remember
that you must give an account to God for everything you do.*
ECCLESIASTES 11:9 NLT

ARE WE THERE YET?

My father taught me not to overthink things, that nothing will
ever be perfect, so just keep moving and do your best.

SCOTT EASTWOOD

Hitting the road with your family changes the routine of work/
homework/practice/cooking. You don't need a lot of money
or a fancy destination to get away and relax. Just make sure that
when you do, you change it up.

Figure out what your family likes to do. Are you the kind
who likes to ride every ride and see every sight, or are you more
in favor of chilling in a new locale, sampling local cuisine, and
doing a few cool things while you're there?

Family trips can be exhausting if you think of them as
an attempt to relax yourself, but when you go and do things
together—travel together, go to the beach together, watch
fireworks together—you build lasting memories and show that
real value and enjoyment come from being together.

*Tell them to go after God, who piles on all the riches we could
ever manage—to do good, to be rich in helping others, to be
extravagantly generous. If they do that, they'll build a
treasury that will last, gaining life that is truly life.*

1 TIMOTHY 6:18–19 MSG

179

YOUR WORD IS YOUR BOND

Your son and your daughter need an excellent father
more than an excellent college.
NICK VUJICIC

Maybe you've had an exchange with your kid that ends with these words: "But Dad, you said. . . !" Kids are quick to let you know when you've disappointed them, and even though that both annoys you and makes you feel terrible, it's important to consider whether they have a point.

Sometimes extenuating circumstances prevent you from fulfilling a promise. You can't take your daughter to the park if the dishwasher is flooding the kitchen. She may complain, but can you apologize and set a new time for the park without her doubting you'll do it?

Making your kid a promise is a sacred thing. When you say you'll be there, move heaven and earth to do it. It's a matter of your own integrity as a man and even more so as a dad. Keeping promises to your kids teaches them integrity in a real and practical way. Doing so builds a foundation for trust and respect that leads to reliability.

My covenant I will not break, nor alter the
word that has gone out of My lips.
PSALM 89:34 NKJV

FAMILY DEVOTIONS

*A man ought to live so that everybody knows he is a
Christian. . .and most of all, his family ought to know.*
Dwight L. Moody

What do you picture when you think of leading your family in devotions? Everyone gathered around your favorite armchair, eyes fixed on you, pin-drop quiet as you dispense prayerfully curated and wisely dispensed biblical gems?

You should set a more realistic expectation. Family devotions won't be as regular as you'd like, last as long as you'd hoped, or go without distractions or interruptions.

But it's better to stumble through than to give up because the reality doesn't match the ideal image in your mind. Many great age-appropriate resources are available. Younger kids like colorfully depicted stories. Older ones appreciate animated resources such as The Bible Project. Start with a worship song, pick an interesting topic, and keep it short. Stick with it; it's worth the craziness!

*Write these commandments that I've given you today on
your hearts. Get them inside of you and then get them inside
your children. Talk about them wherever you are,
sitting at home or walking in the street.*
Deuteronomy 6:6–7 msg

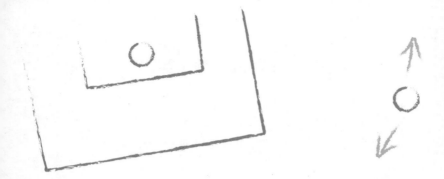

SESSION 7 PLAYBOOK 1:

Loving Your Son

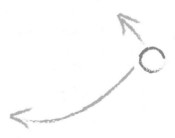

LOVE DANGEROUSLY

My father used to play with my brother and me in the yard.
Mother would come out and say, "You're tearing
up the grass." "We're not raising grass,"
Dad would reply. "We're raising boys."

HARMON KILLEBREW

There's something really cool about raising a son. You may
or may not be the boss at work or a leader at church, but
you're *the man* at home. You're the guy your son looks to when
he wants to see how a man handles life.

In general, then, just being the best man you can be helps
you guide your son into godly manhood. Keep being a servant,
keep loving his mom, keep being present in his life.

Show him the risks of loving well—love dangerously, fostering
healthy competition but allowing for mistakes and redos. Offer
him independence and teach him safe risk-taking and the value
of self-discipline.

You take your example from Jesus, and your son will start
by taking his from you—and then in God's time, he'll become
God's man.

Like arrows in the hand of a warrior, so are the children
of one's youth. Happy is the man who has his quiver
full of them; they shall not be ashamed.
PSALM 127:4–5 NKJV

NO MEANS "NO"

A father is a man who expects his son to
be as good a man as he meant to be.

FRANK A. CLARK

Actions have consequences. Firm, consistent discipline sets boundaries and expectations, and your son needs those. He may bristle when discipline happens, but he will thank you later.

Establish God's objective standards of right and wrong, and take your son to the relevant verses to show him that this whole Christian thing isn't something you just came up with or follow mindlessly. Make sure he understands the concept of sowing and reaping, a spiritual law that can work for or against him.

Show your son how to treat women. Start by loving his mom well, but be deliberate in letting him know that how you love her is no accident but is in response to what God has told you to do.

Do all you can to disrupt entitlement. The things your son enjoys in life are not his birthright but the provision of God, including a family that loves him and leads in God's ways.

Love does no harm to a neighbor.
Therefore love is the fulfillment of the law.

ROMANS 13:10 NIV

RESPECT THE GAME,
RESPECT THE PLAYER

Anyone can be a father, but it takes someone
special to be a dad. . . . You taught me the game,
and you taught me how to play it right.
WADE BOGGS

As men, we tend to speak less, sometimes because we have nothing to say. But when something needs to be said, we need to say it, because our sons are listening.

Don't assume your son will just figure things out. As men, we also feel uncertainty about who we're supposed to be and what we're supposed to do. Many times when things go well, we feel like we're putting one over on somebody because we're not sure how to repeat our success. Let your son hear you talk about things like that.

Despite cultural images to the contrary, men need love too. Show your son that God made men to be a powerful blend of tough and tender. He can be tough around the guys but should be able to cry on the way home with you.

*I am not writing these things to shame you, but to warn you
as my beloved children. . . . So I urge you to imitate me.*
1 CORINTHIANS 4:14, 16 NLT

RAISING A HERO

You don't raise heroes, you raise sons. And if you treat
them like sons, they'll turn out to be heroes,
even if it's just in your own eyes.
WALTER M. SCHIRRA SR.

When he was little, your son believed you could do anything. When he watched superhero cartoons, he thought it was entirely possible you could be hiding a secret identity and going out to fight crime after you tucked him in for the night.

Stay intentional about modeling that standard for your son. Be positive, especially when there's a conflict—with a teacher, a neighbor, a coach, even his mom if there's a divorce.

Teach him the game, but let him win sometimes—just to show him that big things are possible. Model how to deal with losing; he doesn't have to like it, but he can learn from it. Hug him a lot when he's little, and he'll let you do it when he's older. Affirm him when he's little, and he'll believe you when he's older. Listen when he's little, and he'll still share when he's not.

"For the LORD your God is going with you! He will fight for you against your enemies, and he will give you victory!"
DEUTERONOMY 20:4 NLT

LETTING HIM DRIVE

When I was a kid, I used to imagine animals running under
my bed. I told my dad, and he solved the problem
quickly. He cut the legs off the bed.

UNKNOWN

Boys need certain things: advance notice on everything, for
starters. Your boy needs food, so learn to recognize when
he's hangry, and feed him to calm him down. Avoid lecturing him;
discuss issues instead. He needs physical activity, both for health
and to burn off steam.

Provide examples for your son's chores ("This is a clean
sock. This is a dirty sock"). Remember his competitive nature;
make sure he knows you're on his team. When he's little, let him
pretend to drive on your lap.

Bring your son into your thought processes and experiences
as a dad. Let him know that you want to be a great dad, that
you want to provide an example of what it means to follow God
and love your family and others well. Give him permission to
call you out when you fall short. A key part of godly discipline
is discipling, after all.

Correct your son, and he will give you comfort;
he will also delight your soul.
PROVERBS 29:17 NASB

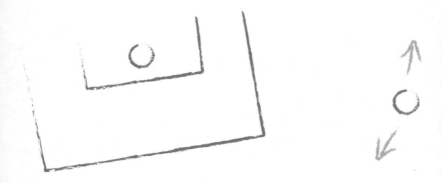

SESSION 7 PLAYBOOK 2:

Loving Your Daughter

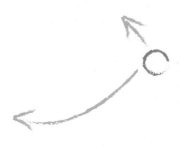

HER FIRST LOVE

Dads are most ordinary men turned by love into heroes,
adventurers, story-tellers, singers of songs.

PAM BROWN

Dads today are more involved in caring for their kids than ever.
The days of dropping off the pregnant wife at the hospital
curb and smoking in the waiting room are long gone, and that's
for the better. Dads get in on the action from day one—changing
diapers, giving baths, putting baby down to sleep, and getting
up in the middle of the night to calm her down.

The beauty of that is a stronger sense of investment for the
dad, but even more wonderful is that your daughter knows from
her first memories the comfort of your presence.

Let those early contributions become your way of life. You
can demonstrate that dads loving their wives and kids and being
there for them is the way things should be. She'll learn in time
that's not how the world is, but let that be a surprise to her.

*Jesus said, "Let the children alone, and do not hinder
them from coming to Me; for the kingdom of
heaven belongs to such as these."*
MATTHEW 19:14 NASB

UNCONDITIONAL AFFECTION

> When I come home, my daughter will run to the door
> and give me a big hug, and everything that's
> happened that day just melts away.
>
> HUGH JACKMAN

When your girl is little, physical affection is a regular thing—hugs and kisses and sitting on your lap. But as she gets older, she still needs that affection from you. It might feel strange to you, especially as she hits adolescence and starts turning into a little woman, but if you don't maintain that unconditional affection, someone else will fill the void—and not without conditions.

Let her know that boundaries are necessary and that she has the right to be loved without a guy expecting anything in return. She needs to know that "no" means no, and the fatherly affection she gets from you sets the tone for that expectation.

Dance with your daughter, take her on dates, and model for her what to expect from a boy who claims to like her. As writer Jim Bishop said, "Watching your daughter being collected for her first date feels like handing over a million-dollar Stradivarius to a gorilla."

> *Charm is deceptive, and beauty does not last;*
> *but a woman who fears the LORD will be greatly praised.*
> PROVERBS 31:30 NLT

SAVE A WALL; BUILD A BRIDGE

When my father didn't have my hand, he had my back.
LINDA POINDEXTER

Your daughter needs to know she can come to you with anything and everything. Set that expectation as early as possible. It may not come as naturally to you as it does with your son, but it's every bit as important.

Be firm but gentle. You're her role model for manhood, so forming those bonds with her is crucial. Because of your warm bonds, she will drive you nuts at times and try to manipulate you—and you will be tempted to comply. Resist. She needs you to hold that line for her.

When your daughter comes to you with a problem, you will automatically go into problem-solving mode. Shut it off for the time being and instead ask yourself, *What is she feeling right now?* Be an active listener; pay attention to her body language—her expressions, tone, and mood—and don't rush to conclusions. Just listen. It shows you care.

"Stand at the crossroads and look; ask for the ancient paths, ask where the good way is, and walk in it, and you will find rest for your souls."
JEREMIAH 6:16 NIV

THE GIFT OF BELIEF

*My father gave me the greatest gift anyone could
give another person. . .he believed in me.*
JIM VALVANO

Make time to listen. Take time every day just to sit with your daughter in her room and let her talk about whatever she wants to talk about. And if she asks about your day, you share too. Take her seriously as someone who can learn and grow—teach her to fish, shoot a jump shot, put together a shelf, change a flat, and put up a tent.

Girls feel a ton of pressure to look a certain way, and even if their inclination is to resist it, all girls want to feel like they're beautiful. Make sure your daughter knows that's exactly how you see her.

Even more importantly, affirm her courage, loyalty, intelligence, grit, and humor. God always looks for inner beauty over appearance, and so should you. As her dad, you've already got her heart, but you should always be trying to win it. Cherish her, prefer her, and pray for and with her.

*You should clothe yourselves instead with the beauty that
comes from within, the unfading beauty of a gentle
and quiet spirit, which is so precious to God.*
1 PETER 3:4 NLT

A STRONG SHELTER

Having a daughter makes you see things in a different way. . . .
As long as you treat her the same way I treat
her, like my princess, I don't mind.
TRACY MORGAN

Does your daughter know she is your princess? Is she aware that not only do you love her and think she's beautiful, but you believe she is capable of great things? Does she sleep better knowing that you would crawl across blazing sand dunes to rescue her—and that you will have her back at a parent-teacher conference too? Make sure she is on stable footing in all of these areas, and she will be able to overcome all the pressure she feels from the world around her to be and do certain things.

Be intentional in building up your daughter. Even if you're confident you can answer yes to all the questions above, talk to your daughter about life. Guide her in the whys of what's right and wrong, teaching discernment and the importance of limits and correction. Your love shelters her from the world and prepares her to trust God.

GOD's name is a place of protection—
good people can run there and be safe.
PROVERBS 18:10 MSG

STRATEGY SESSION 8:

REAL ACCOUNTABILITY

FAITH WALKING

A truly rich man is one whose children run into
his arms when his hands are empty.
UNKNOWN

Walking in faith means looking past the time-stamped things of the world and seeking God's ways instead. It means keeping perspective on all the criticism you encounter as you go—from all directions, including from your own mind—and looking for what God has to say. It means being prepared to look foolish because people don't understand what you're doing.

It's admitting you can't do anything without God (John 15:5), asking God for help (Psalm 50:15), and being grateful for what you have (Psalm 106:1). If you believe what you say you believe, you'll always come back to one basic question: *Is what I'm doing pleasing to God?*

Walking in faith is trusting God with your parenting. It's planting seeds in your children's hearts and trusting the Holy Spirit to water them. It's being fundamentally aware that God knows and loves your kids even more than you do. It's keeping your door and arms open when your kids mess up and letting God love them through you.

The LORD knows the days of the upright,
and their inheritance shall be forever.
PSALM 37:18 NKJV

HABITS OF HAPPINESS

> I heard a story of two farmers praying to God for rain
> to come. Both prayed but only one prepared the land.
> Who do you think trusted God more to send the rain?
>
> Mr. Bridges, *Facing the Giants*

A life of faith involves the regular practice of remembering things about God you've forgotten through disuse. When you feel like He isn't listening to you, keep praying. He hears you and has your good in mind—and the good of many others your prayers will affect in ways you can't imagine.

When you feel out of your depth, remember that God gives wisdom freely. When you don't feel like worshipping, worship anyway. When you feel out of sorts, seek God in His Word, accept what He shows you there, and apply it to your life.

When your kids aren't walking with the Lord, you keep walking. See if there's anything you could be doing better, but then remember that your kids are individuals with their own personalities, wills, and responsibility to respond to God. Do your humble best and trust God to do His.

> *I could have no greater joy than to hear that
> my children are following the truth.*
>
> 3 John 4 NLT

THE LIMITS OF WILLPOWER

I smile because you are my father. I laugh because
there's nothing you can do about it.
UNKNOWN

Your kids will drive you crazy at various times and for various reasons. You will have times when you wonder, *Where did I go wrong?* There's no easy answer to that question—not because you're a royal flop as a dad but because your determination to raise them well is not the cause-and-effect situation you'd like it to be.

Don't give up (Galatians 6:9). Keep practicing self-control, because once your kids get over their bad selves (which usually doesn't happen until their midtwenties or so), they'll look back and realize you were onto something.

Self-control is the ultimate fruit of the Spirit, the cherry on top of the Christian sundae. Your ongoing fight against the carnal thoughts of your heart and mind, the lusts of your body, and the temptations of destructive old habits is worth the struggle. God is faithful. While you or your kids can come up short, God never does and never will.

For the Spirit God gave us does not make us timid,
but gives us power, love and self-discipline.
2 TIMOTHY 1:7 NIV

ONE PIECE AT A TIME

[Winning] starts with complete command of the fundamentals. Then it takes desire, determination, discipline, and self-sacrifice. And finally, it takes a great deal of love, fairness, and respect for your fellow man.

JESSE OWENS

Dissatisfaction with the goals you've set is often a holy indicator that you need to get back to basics, fully trusting God and seeking Him in prayer and His Word. If you lack direction, turn toward God. Ask Him to intervene with a verse that speaks to your heart or a person with a message for you. Set goals that guide you back to Him.

Wait on God and consult with Him as you make plans. Be patient and trust His timing. Realize that His work in you is a lifelong process. Keep your priorities in order, and a direction will open up for you to take another step—with the overarching goal of drawing closer to God.

"Oh, that You would bless me indeed, and enlarge my territory, that Your hand would be with me, and that You would keep me from evil, that I may not cause pain!"
So God granted him what he requested.
1 CHRONICLES 4:10 NKJV

ROUTINE MAINTENANCE

The big things that come our way. . .are the fruit of
seeds planted in the daily routine of your work.
WILLIAM FEATHER

Establishing a routine for your children helps you organize your time and priorities. There are many good reasons to set up a regular schedule for your kids.

When they're babies, it helps them get on a schedule, which is good for everyone's health and sanity. As kids get older, they look to traditions and routines as sources of security and comfort. If family devotions are part of the routine, studying the Bible will seem normal and even fun.

Knowing what to expect is crucial for kids. Being able to rely on certain things happening around certain times reduces stress and worry—and when things get out of whack, getting back into the routine can restore peace and calm. You foster confidence and independence when you let your kids know what's coming and how to deal with it. They can get through a hard day by looking forward to the time they'll have with you.

O God, thou art my God; early will I seek thee:
my soul thirsteth for thee.
PSALM 63:1 KJV

GODLINESS IN, GARBAGE OUT

We first make our habits, and then our habits make us.
JOHN DRYDEN

Stress and boredom are kindling for a lot of bad habits. Life always includes varying forms of stress, but boredom usually means your spiritual life needs a spark. However, you don't need something new and shiny—a new Bible, a new church, a new men's group, a new book. You just need to get back to the tried and true.

If your devotional time has gotten stale, try a new approach, but don't abandon meditating on scripture and asking God to help you know Him better. Boredom with God isn't possible. It's just that you've gotten bored with your view of God, which more often than not limits Him to what you think He is or can do.

You don't get rid of bad habits; you replace them. Once you're aware of a problem and what triggers it, then make it hard to do. Replace it with something better.

Be renewed in the spirit of your mind, and put on the new self, which in the likeness of God has been created in righteousness and holiness of the truth.
EPHESIANS 4:23–24 NASB

TEND YOUR GARDEN

Before you act, listen. Before you react, think. Before you
spend, earn. Before you criticize, wait. Before you
pray, forgive. Before you quit, try.
ERNEST HEMINGWAY

Slipping into bad habits in your closest relationships happens
easily. If you find yourself getting along better with people
outside your home than the ones in it, it's time to take a look at
what's going on with your family. If things are dragging between
you and your loved ones, take the initiative to get interactions
flowing again.

If you keep having the same argument with your kids, you
haven't dealt with the issue at the heart of it. Resolve it with
your kids in a calm moment. Also, don't take them for granted.
Affirmation and gratitude are always welcome.

As the expert on your family, you're aware of each of your
kids' preferences and tendencies. You may not like or understand
those inclinations, but knowing them can help you build (or re-
build) rapport. Love them in ways that speak to their hearts. Deal
with issues as soon as you can, and ask God to help you do so.

A friend loves at all times, and a brother is born for adversity.
PROVERBS 17:17 NKJV

CRUEL TO BE KIND

The greatest gift a parent can give a child is unconditional
love. As a child wanders and strays, finding his bearings,
he needs a sense of absolute love from a parent.
There's nothing wrong with tough love,
as long as the love is unconditional.

GEORGE W. BUSH

Tough love is being willing to have hard conversations with your kids when they've gotten off course. It's refusing to enable bad choices and calling your children to a higher standard. It's being truthful when telling a lie would be easier. It's letting natural consequences play out without intervening to bear the blow. As the term indicates, it's hard to do and it always starts and ends with love.

The Bible mentions speaking the truth in love (Ephesians 4:15). You need to bring both, because truth without love is harsh and love without truth is insincere. True love requires truth. You do the hard things because you love your kids and want them to be prepared for adult life. You hold the line because God has drawn it and you want them to understand that His boundaries are for their protection.

As iron sharpens iron, so a friend sharpens a friend.
PROVERBS 27:17 NLT

SHARE YOUR STORIES

Of all the titles I've been privileged to have,
"Dad" has always been the best.
KEN NORTON

One of the most important things you do as a dad is to lead your kids by example. That includes preparing them for the realities of adult life, where mistakes and disappointments are not in short supply. Your kids need to know that they can and should learn from their mistakes, that doing so actually makes them better at making decisions. There's no better example to offer than your own stories of blunders and miscalculations.

You may have done some things as a young person that you definitely don't want your kids doing. And your kids may play the "Well, *you* did it" card.

Explain that when you were their age, you weren't looking at things through the lens of being a father. Point out that just because you turned out all right doesn't mean they will. Focus on God's faithfulness and how His prohibitions are for their safety.

We will not hide them from their children, telling to the
generation to come the praises of the LORD, and His
strength and His wonderful works that He has done.
PSALM 78:4 NKJV

TAKING OWNERSHIP

What we desire our children to become,
we must endeavor to be before them.
ANDREW COMBE

You know you're in the dad business for real when your children start playing the blaming game. You see the results across the culture—it seems like everyone plays the victim, blaming someone else for what's wrong with their lives. Your mission, should you choose to accept it: uproot blame and victimization in your home as soon as you see them creeping in.

Teach your kids to take ownership. They need to know that each of us is responsible for our own behavior. They win when they admit they're wrong and lose when they make excuses (you can even keep count if that resonates with your kids).

You have to help your kids replace bad habits with good ones, so show them the value of conflict resolution and model it in your interactions with them. When you accept responsibility for your own actions, seeking forgiveness and restoration, that will help you find a starting point for them to follow your example.

The godly walk with integrity;
blessed are their children who follow them.
PROVERBS 20:7 NLT

THE GOAL IS UNITY

Remember not only to say the right thing in the right place,
but far more difficult still, to leave unsaid the
wrong thing at the tempting moment.
BENJAMIN FRANKLIN

Conflict is inevitable, so be sure to handle it biblically, with relational growth and improved unity as potential outcomes.

Jesus called us to be peacemakers: "You're blessed when you can show people how to cooperate instead of compete or fight. That's when you discover who you really are, and your place in God's family" (Matthew 5:9 MSG). That's not an automatic response to conflict, however; it requires deliberate forethought, prayer, and practice.

Model this approach: Define the issue and stick to it. Face up to your own problems before addressing those of others. Plan a time to talk, rather than dealing with an issue on the fly. Share your feelings and give the other person the same opportunity. Make sure restoring relationships is your top priority.

Be agreeable, be sympathetic, be loving, be compassionate,
be humble. That goes for all of you, no exceptions.
No retaliation. No sharp-tongued sarcasm. Instead,
bless—that's your job, to bless. You'll be a
blessing and also get a blessing.
1 PETER 3:8–9 MSG

HONORING CAUSE AND EFFECT

Obedience to God's will is the secret of
spiritual knowledge and insight.
ERIC LIDDELL

When it comes to your role in forming your children's character, you don't get any days off. It's like pedaling uphill—the minute you stop, you start slipping backward. You can stock the shelves of their moral warehouses, but unless they use the products, the shelf life is short.

The world bombards all of God's people with false philosophies—self-sufficiency, materialism, atheism, and so on. Even though the results of those worldviews are evident in the horrors of the news, we can still become desensitized—and that's dangerous, since God has called us to be salt and light to the world.

Keep your approaches practical with your kids. Help them figure out how to follow God's rules. Discuss or list their options and the consequences. Cue them toward compliance with written reminders posted around the house—lists of rules or encouraging verses. Think of it as posting your family's mission statement. Discuss consequences, and then enforce them. Stick to God's way, and He will bless your parenting and your family.

*Remember, it is sin to know what you
ought to do and then not do it.*
JAMES 4:17 NLT

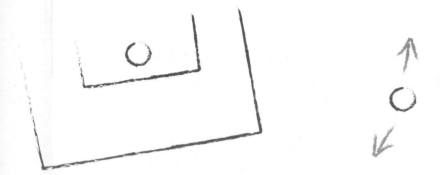

SESSION 8 PLAYBOOK:

Emotional Intelligence

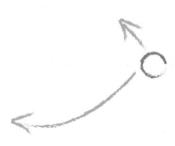

THIS IS THE FOREST;
THESE ARE THE TREES

*No one cares how much you know,
until they know how much you care.*
THEODORE ROOSEVELT

Though it sounds kind of newfangled, emotional intelligence is a vital concept for your success as a father. Emotional intelligence is a blend of your IQ, EQ (emotional quotient), and personality. It reflects biblical wisdom in its concepts of self-awareness and self-control. Emotion drives behavior (even though we think it doesn't), so when you recognize, understand, and manage your emotions, you can improve your behavior.

Higher EQ improves relationships through increased empathy (understanding another's feelings and frame of reference) and self-awareness (knowing how you see yourself and how others see you). It helps you keep the big picture in mind while still paying attention to the details. You can imagine the applications for your parenting.

An increasingly complex world demands game-changing approaches in raising your kids. Filtered through a biblical lens, strengthening your emotional intelligence will help you prepare your kids to serve God and others with compassion, peace, and resilience.

*Instruct the wise and they will be wiser still;
teach the righteous and they will add to their learning.*
PROVERBS 9:9 NIV

WHERE DOES IT HURT?

How far you go in life depends on your being tender with
the young, compassionate with the aged, sympathetic with
the striving, and tolerant of the weak and strong.
Because someday in your life you
will have been all of these.
GEORGE WASHINGTON CARVER

Because we are created in God's image, all human beings are
wired for empathy. God demonstrated empathy by becoming
one of us in order to show us the way back to Him.

Empathy works on two levels: one, feeling what others feel,
either by detecting their feelings or mirroring them, and two,
being able to take their perspective to understand their feelings. Sometimes it happens naturally, but in some it's cultivated
through experience.

Your model is critical to your children's ability to maintain
empathy. Show compassion for others, assume the best about
others' intentions, be respectful when resolving an issue, apologize when necessary, and practice patience while out and
about. Most of all, make sure they know about Jesus, the perfect
example of empathy and comfort.

*Let each of you look out not only for his own interests,
but also for the interests of others.*
PHILIPPIANS 2:4 NKJV

A SATISFIED MIND

I have no special talents; I am only passionately curious.

ALBERT EINSTEIN

Teaching your children to love learning is a lifelong gift. God meant for us to explore and take interest in this world. Even if your kids don't love school, they can still find areas of interest and pursue them, and you can coach them in doing so.

Be a keen observer. Watch what they do and listen to what they say. Look for what holds their interest and what doesn't. Listen to their ideas, not to see if they're wrong or right, but to look for original thinking. You want them to be thinkers, not blindly tolerant of any opinion that presents itself. On moral issues, lead them back to scripture.

Model your own pursuit of learning. When you get excited about a ladybug or a cloud formation, you demonstrate the joy of discovery. God has a great adventure for your children, and learning about His world will point them back to Him on a regular basis.

"Call to Me and I will answer you, and I will tell you great and mighty things, which you do not know."

JEREMIAH 33:3 NASB

WHAT LIGHTS YOUR FIRE?

Faith gives you a concept of the dignity and worth of all work,
even simple work, without which work could bore you.

TIM KELLER

Habitually looking for the deeper questions and issues enriches your interactions with your kids. In the Sermon on
the Mount (Matthew 5), Jesus used the touchstone "You have
heard that it was said. . .but I say to you. . . ." He distinguished
between superficial religious activity that made people feel good
about themselves, as opposed to God's intention behind the law.

You can develop the habit of deeper thinking by regularly
engaging in in-depth study of the Bible. When you read scripture
and ask not just what it's saying but what it means (and what it
means to you), you're searching for deeper truth.

Deep thinkers process info, comparing it with what they
already know to see if there are ways to improve. These are
problem solvers who always ask why—why we do what we do, why
it matters, why we exist—and the result is that living a righteous
life matters to them.

*You desire truth in the innermost being, and in the hidden
part You will make me know wisdom.*
PSALM 51:6 NASB

UNDER CONSTRUCTION

We have a right to believe whatever we want,
but not everything we believe is right.
RAVI ZACHARIAS

Faith matters, as well as what or who you place it in and whether or not you put it into action. Researchers have found a link between emotional intelligence and religious belief—but only for those who take their faith seriously. They found no correlation between emotional intelligence and the outward appearance of religiosity.

James could have told them as much when he said, "Faith without works is useless" (James 2:20 NASB). When you reserve the Gospel for Sunday sermons and small-group discussion, it's like holding back a cure for a deadly disease. When you put hands and feet on the Gospel, it changes lives. To lead yourself and your family, you need to act on the belief that God is real; that He is holy, loving, and merciful; and that He will hold you accountable for how you respond to Jesus.

Do not conform to the pattern of this world, but be transformed by the renewing of your mind. Then you will be able to test and approve what God's will is—his good, pleasing and perfect will.
ROMANS 12:2 NIV

ONCE MORE, WITH FEELING

God desires to be loved by men, although He needs them
not; and men refuse to love God, though they
need Him in an infinite degree.
UNKNOWN

Being intentional means more than just doing things on purpose instead of accidentally. It hinges on learning about your emotions—both what the Bible says and the latest scientific findings (to see if they corroborate scripture; if not, set them aside).

Learn how your mind works—where you tend to go on autopilot and if that's good or not. Fight-or-flight, for example, can be a good response if it pulls your kids out of danger, but it's less useful in dealing with stress or conflict.

Be committed to your and your family's growth on every level—physical, mental, emotional, and spiritual. Doing so takes energy and focus, along with preparation and attention.

With clear lines drawn, priorities will clarify, from meeting basic needs (safety, shelter, and sustenance) to wants such as a bigger house, newer car, or the latest phone. You'll find it easier to set and accomplish goals.

You ask and do not receive, because you ask with wrong
motives, so that you may spend it on your pleasures.
JAMES 4:3 NASB

BEING INSPIRED MAKES
YOU INSPIRING

*A passion for God isn't necessarily the same as abiding in God;
it must be coupled with obedience to be true love for God.*

<small>EDWIN LOUIS COLE</small>

A passion for people or a subject becomes contagious and drives what you do. It's like a God-given instinct that energizes and sustains you, rubs off on others, and helps them persevere through thick and thin.

Passion begins with loving God with all you are. You can't love someone like that without knowing them. This ties in with being intentional about wanting to know God more and better. You get to know Him by reading the Bible. As you read, ask yourself, *What was God thinking or feeling here?* Doing so will open up your mind to His passion for relationship.

Take that passion you feel for your kids and let it motivate you to hang in there when the going gets tough. If they see that your fierce love for them motivates you in all you do, they will respond in positive ways—sometimes immediately, but mostly over time.

*God is working in you, giving you the desire
and the power to do what pleases him.*

<small>PHILIPPIANS 2:13 NLT</small>

GET BETTER OR GROW BITTER

We cannot change our past. . . . The only thing we can do is
play on the one string we have, and that is our attitude.
CHUCK SWINDOLL

Attitude is always within your control, and when you control it, you're happier, more motivated, and more successful.

Gratitude is a good focal point. Think about what you have rather than what you don't. Count your blessings. Being rich means much more than having money. Appreciating what God has done for you gives you confidence that He will continue to take care of you. Satisfaction results, which leaves emotional room to connect and listen.

Your relationship with your children is more than just a role you're playing. Do your best to understand them, and make your expectations clear. With each child's uniqueness and limitations in mind, work on solutions, not punishment. You can be genuine about hardship without sacrificing the optimism that comes from knowing that God is bigger than your problems. Your kids need to see that from you.

Hope does not disappoint, because the love of God has
been poured out within our hearts through
the Holy Spirit who was given to us.
ROMANS 5:5 NASB

JUST KEEP SWIMMING

Even if you are on the right track,
you will get run over if you just sit there!
WILL ROGERS

I n life, change is constant. Do you know when to hold course and when to change it? God is the only constant, and if He is your true worth, you'll be able to figure out whether to press on in your current direction or switch it up.

Letting things go and trusting that God will continue to provide takes courage and flexibility. Sometimes it's a job you thought you'd always have, and other times it's a relationship you always thought you could count on. Faith is not about understanding every move God makes but about believing in Him enough to make your own move when He leads you down a different path.

It's true with your kids too. If one strategy isn't working, try something else. Stay open to possibilities and new ways of seeing and thinking about a situation. You can always change.

Because of Jesus, starting over is always an option.

"You will keep him in perfect peace, whose mind is stayed on You, because he trusts in You."
ISAIAH 26:3 NKJV

TWO IMPOSTERS

> If you can meet with Triumph and Disaster and treat
> those two impostors just the same. . . .
> RUDYARD KIPLING

God teaches us more through disaster than triumph. How you handle your children's failure is more important than how you handle their success.

Let your kid be a kid. Give her the gift of letting her learn from her experiences. Play and laugh with her. Be patient when she makes mistakes, but step in when she needs help or redirection. She will respect the boundaries you set up, especially if she knows you're invested in loving her.

God is all about second chances. Your children can start with a clean slate, and it helps when you tell them that beating themselves up for past choices doesn't help and that such action is not what you—or God—are looking for. He is interested not just in His glory but in their benefit. He can use both success and failure to help them love Him more.

> *If anyone is in Christ, he is a new creation; old things have
> passed away; behold, all things have become new.*
> 2 CORINTHIANS 5:17 NKJV

THE STORM BEFORE THE CALM

Anyone can be angry—that is easy. But to be angry with the right person, to the right degree, at the right time, for the right purpose, and in the right way—that is not easy.

ARISTOTLE

Despite your best efforts to remain cool and calm, there will be times when your child does or says something that has the effect of a keyboard mash—pressing all your buttons at once! You might need to, in military parlance, go dark for a while so you can calm down and deal with the situation.

If it helps, treat the situation as an emergency—like when your kid does something dumb and gets hurt and ends up in the ER. You don't berate him; you switch into protector and caretaker mode and resolve to deal with the stupid part later.

God can help you regulate your emotions, including disappointment. Don't worry that your kid doesn't understand that he's done something foolish. He just needs to know that you still love him no matter what.

"No weapon forged against you will prevail, and you will refute every tongue that accuses you. This is the heritage of the servants of the LORD, and this is their vindication from me," declares the LORD.

ISAIAH 54:17 NIV

OUR GREATEST NEED

There is more mercy in Christ than sin in us.
RICHARD SIBBES

God sent Jesus as our Savior because He knew that what we needed most was forgiveness. One of the Holy Spirit's jobs is to convict us of our sin and convince us of our need for forgiveness, and you show great sensitivity to Him when you extend this same mercy to your kids.

To show your kids the power of forgiveness, help them understand the difference between an apology and a request for forgiveness. When you say you're sorry, you're indicating regret, meaning you feel bad about what you did. But when you ask someone you've wronged to forgive you, you put the ball in his court. It's up to him whether he will forgive you. When you ask God, though, He without a doubt forgives you. And because of that, He wants you to be forgiving with others (Ephesians 4:32).

Grace and forgiveness prevent imperfections from destroying your relationships. Be consistent in teaching your kids the importance of seeking, and giving, forgiveness.

What is desirable in a man is his kindness,
and it is better to be a poor man than a liar.
PROVERBS 19:22 NASB

PERSEVERANCE

Our motto must continue to be perseverance. And ultimately,
I trust the Almighty will crown our efforts with success.

WILLIAM WILBERFORCE

No trait is more richly rewarded in a Christian's life than
perseverance. With it, you will be able to stick with your
goals and live out your beliefs—and fulfill your objective of
raising godly children.

Paul likened perseverance to running a race (1 Corinthians
9:24–27). With the spiritual reward of God's honor and eternal
life awaiting you, you have the inspiration you need. To accomplish your goal, though, you'll need to prepare and pace yourself
so you can finish, and when you hit a wall, you can trust God to
keep you moving.

You're going to fumble; it's part of this life. Expect it, treat it
like a temporary setback, and keep trying. Take the Bible—God's
playbook—to heart and put it into practice. He will strengthen
you to be the dad your kids need and give you relationships with
them that will enrich all your lives.

> *"If you decide that it's a bad thing to worship GOD,*
> *then choose a god you'd rather serve. . . . As for me*
> *and my family, we'll worship GOD."*
> JOSHUA 24:15 MSG

ABOUT THE AUTHOR

Quentin Guy writes from the high desert of New Mexico to encourage and equip people to know and serve God. He currently works in publishing for Calvary Church and has cowritten such books as *Weird and Gross Bible Stuff* and *The 2:52 Boys Bible*, both of which are stuck in future classic status. A former middle school teacher, he serves with his wife as a marriage prep mentor and trusts God that his children will survive their teenage years.

SCRIPTURE INDEX